CAPE COUNTRY

RANDOM HOUSE

UK | USA | Canada | Ireland | Australia
India | New Zealand | South Africa | China

Random House is an imprint of the Penguin Random House group of companies, whose addresses can be found at global.penguinrandomhouse.com.

First published by Penguin Random House New Zealand, 2016

1 3 5 7 9 10 8 6 4 2

Text © Jenny Carlyon and Diana Morrow, 2016
Photography © Richard Brimer, 2016, unless credited otherwise

The moral rights of the authors have been asserted.

All rights reserved. Without limiting the rights under copyright reserved above, no part of this publication may be reproduced, stored in or introduced into a retrieval system, or transmitted, in any form or by any means (electronic, mechanical, photocopying, recording or otherwise), without the prior written permission of both the copyright owner and the above publisher of this book.

Design by Kate Barraclough © Penguin Random House New Zealand
Prepress by Image Centre Group
Printed and bound in China by Leo Paper Products Ltd

A catalogue record for this book is available from the National Library of New Zealand.

ISBN 978-1-77553-881-3

penguin.co.nz

Seven generations of Gordons at Clifton, Cape Kidnappers

CAPE COUNTRY

Jenny Carlyon & Diana Morrow
with Angus Gordon

PHOTOGRAPHY BY RICHARD BRIMER

RANDOM HOUSE
NEW ZEALAND

CONTENTS

- 7   PREFACE
- 11   INTRODUCTION
  Continuum: Seven Generations at Clifton
- 21   CHAPTER ONE
  Beginnings
- 49   CHAPTER TWO
  Founding Clifton
- 79   CHAPTER THREE
  Frank Gordon: Life on the Land
- 113   CHAPTER FOUR
  Testing Times
- 147   CHAPTER FIVE
  Halcyon Years
- 183   CHAPTER SIX
  New Directions
- 229   CHAPTER SEVEN
  Summerlee/Cape Kidnappers: A Remarkable Transformation
- 249   CHAPTER EIGHT
  The Hansens of Haupouri
- 257   CHAPTER NINE
  Creating the Cape Sanctuary
- 291   CONCLUSION
  An Ongoing Legacy
- 296   BIBLIOGRAPHY
- 298   ACKNOWLEDGEMENTS
- 300   INDEX

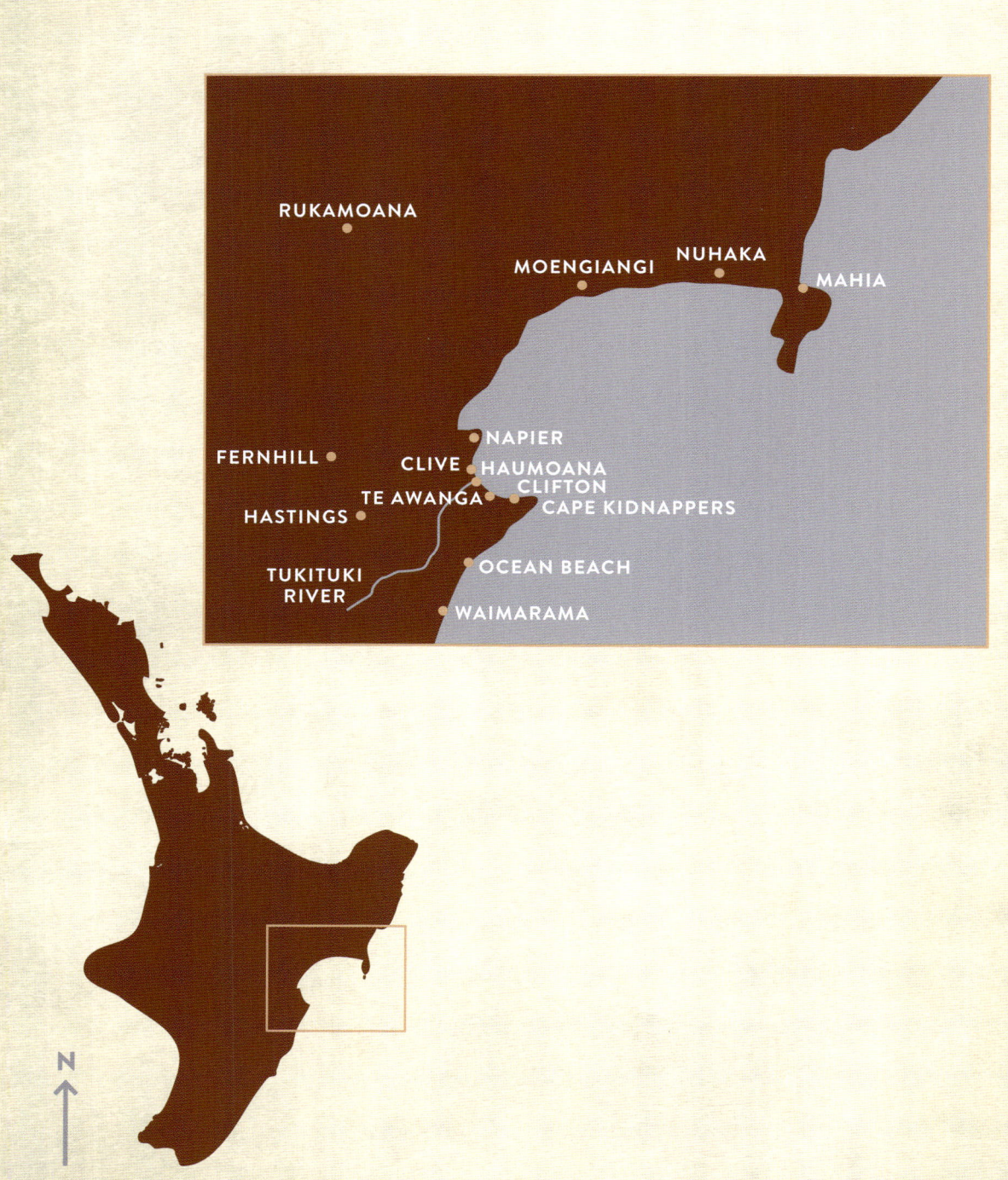

PREFACE

The Gordon family has been at Clifton since 1861. Although farming in this location is often challenging, it is a spectacularly beautiful environment, situated on the east coast of the North Island, just 20 minutes drive south of Napier. The story of Clifton is a story of a family's deep love and connection to that land and their determination to hand it on intact and thriving to succeeding generations. Six generations of Gordons have enjoyed living there, and the seventh has just been born. Each generation has had a deep attachment to this land, both through times of prosperity and success, and through struggles, droughts, floods and economic downturns. Each has successfully maintained and improved the property to hand on to the next generation.

Although Clifton Station is now just over 800 hectares as opposed to the original 13,000 acres (5260 hectares), the property has only ever been owned by the Gordon family. It is currently being farmed by my brother Angus and his son, Tom.

For me, as for my five siblings, growing up at Clifton was paradise. We lived in a large early-Edwardian homestead set in extensive gardens just metres from the beach. Our days were spent riding our ponies out on the farm, helping our dad, swimming in the sea or river during the long hot summers, picnicking, camping out at the Cape, or just lazing around the garden. It was a privileged childhood in an idyllic setting. We all maintain a great attachment to

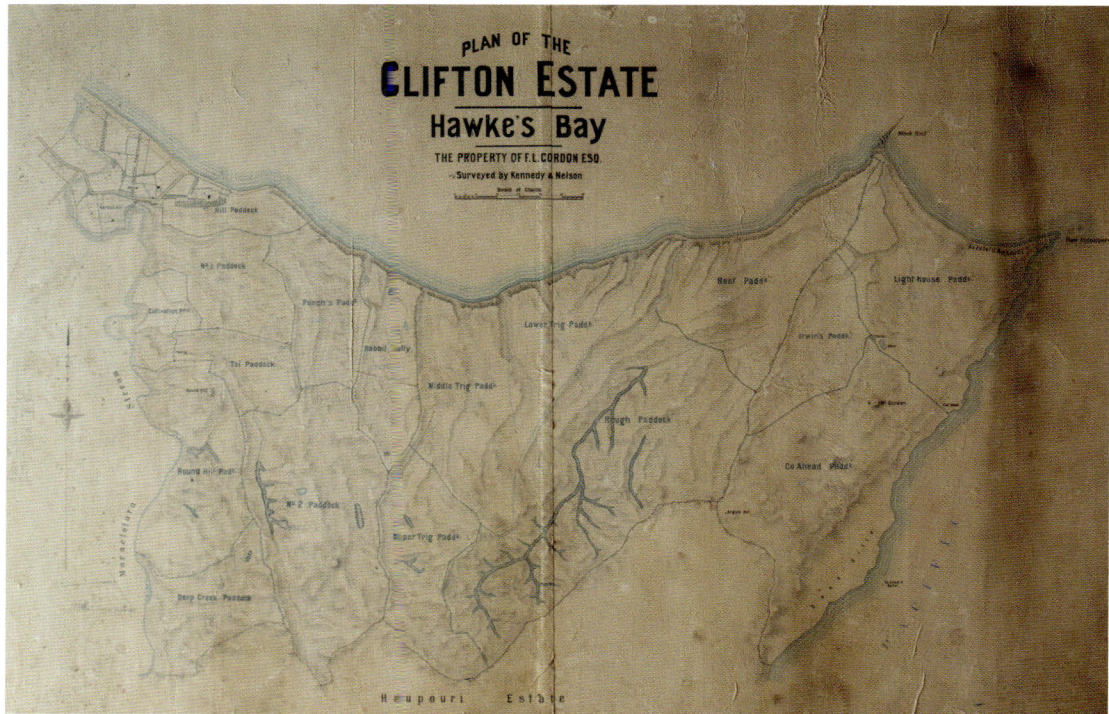

the property. Our own children have also come to love it, as Angus and his wife, Dinah, who continue to live in the homestead, have maintained a tradition of wonderful hospitality for a large extended family of siblings, in-laws, nieces and nephews.

In 2004 Angus published a comprehensive book about the station and its history. Our book, while covering much of the same ground, adds to the story by bringing it up to date with the changes that have taken place not only at Clifton but on the neighbouring properties of Cape Kidnappers and Haupouri, which both once formed part of Clifton Station.

During his time at Clifton, Angus has had to face changing economic and climatic conditions, such as plummeting wool and sheep prices, severe droughts and floods. In this very challenging and changed environment, he has successfully diversified from the traditional income stream of sheep and wool. My co-author Diana Morrow and I have worked together with Angus to tell this story, with its ups and downs, its failures and successes.

As well as delving into the early history of the land, we've also focused on the fourth, fifth and sixth generations of the family to

ABOVE
Plan of Clifton Estate, 1925.
GORDON FAMILY COLLECTION

live at Clifton – John and Barbara, Angus and Dinah, and Tom and Lucia – drawing on extensive interviews with people who worked on the station and with family members: our mother, Barbara, and my five siblings. The book also tells the story of Cape Kidnappers and Haupouri, based on interviews with the landowners – Julian Robertson, Andy Lowe, Robert and Charlotte Fisher, and the Hansen family who are the seventh generation of Gordon descendants at Haupouri – as well as many other people, particularly those involved in the development of the wildlife sanctuary.

All three of these properties are continually transforming and adapting to survive and to meet the demands of modern farming. Their owners have ventured into tourism, cropping, horse rearing, a café, a golf course, and a wildlife sanctuary, while at the same time continuing to farm sheep and cattle. While this book tells the story of this adaption, it is above all the story of one family, the Gordons, who have nurtured and loved the land and made a living out of it for 156 years so far, and hope to be there forever.

Jenny Carlyon

ABOVE
Barbara Gordon and children outside Clifton, 1963.
GORDON FAMILY COLLECTION

INTRODUCTION
CONTINUUM
Seven Generations at Clifton

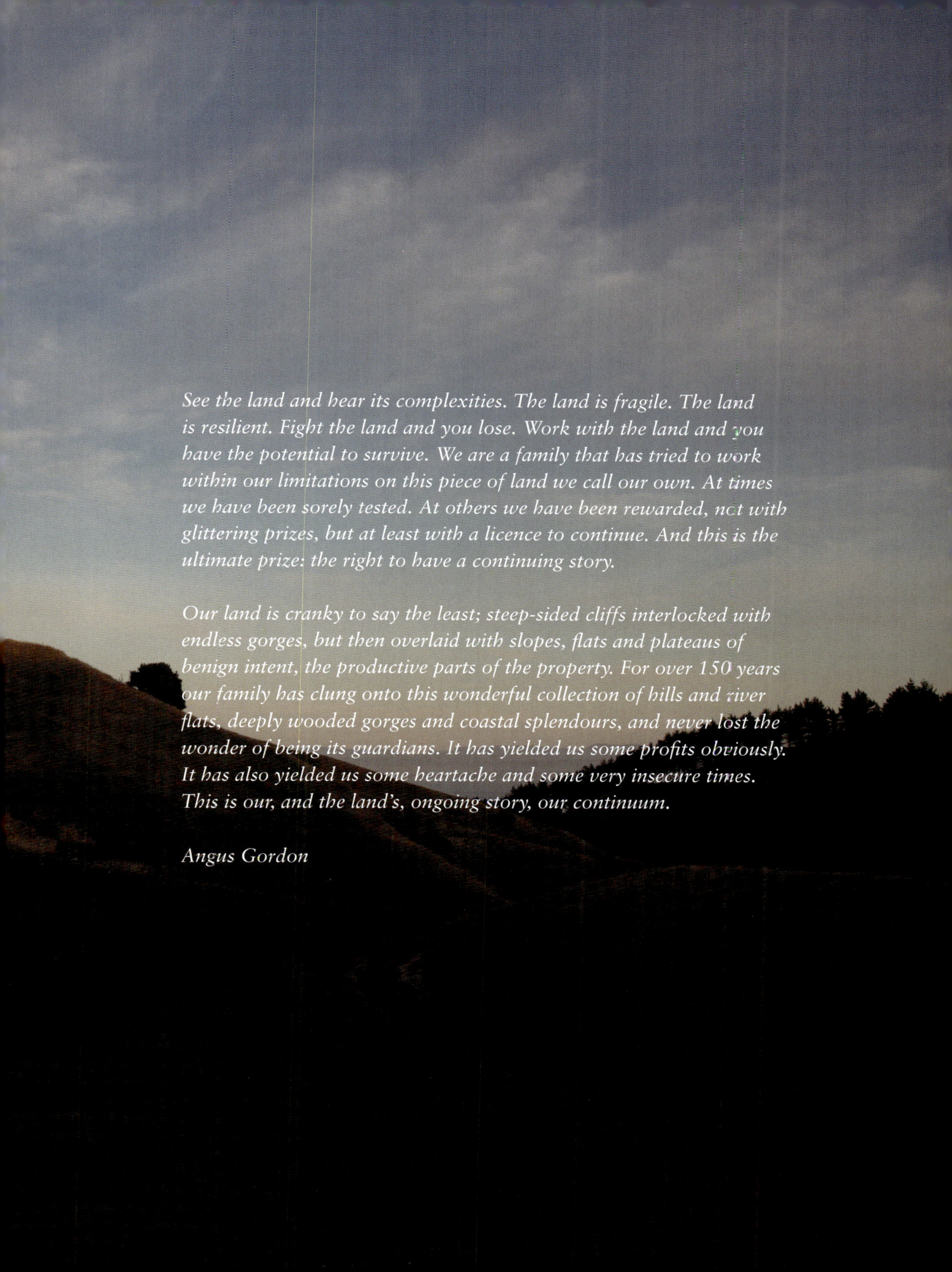

See the land and hear its complexities. The land is fragile. The land is resilient. Fight the land and you lose. Work with the land and you have the potential to survive. We are a family that has tried to work within our limitations on this piece of land we call our own. At times we have been sorely tested. At others we have been rewarded, not with glittering prizes, but at least with a licence to continue. And this is the ultimate prize: the right to have a continuing story.

Our land is cranky to say the least; steep-sided cliffs interlocked with endless gorges, but then overlaid with slopes, flats and plateaus of benign intent, the productive parts of the property. For over 150 years our family has clung onto this wonderful collection of hills and river flats, deeply wooded gorges and coastal splendours, and never lost the wonder of being its guardians. It has yielded us some profits obviously. It has also yielded us some heartache and some very insecure times. This is our, and the land's, ongoing story, our continuum.

Angus Gordon

Angus Gordon is the fifth generation of his family to farm Clifton Station in Hawke's Bay. His son, Tom, who farms it with him, is the sixth. Originally the farm was 13,000 acres (5260 hectares) of wild, rugged, isolated country that included the magnificent Cape Kidnappers headland. Over the years, that acreage has gradually decreased, as blocks were carved off for family members: Taurapa went to Charlie Gordon in 1895, and Haupouri to his brother Edward in 1906. Then in 1924, Angus's grandfather Frank sold the vast Cape block to the Neilson family, who renamed it Summerlee. This land is now known as Cape Kidnappers Station. Angus takes pride in having retained the core of the Clifton property, some 2000 acres (810 hectares). The farm has changed and adapted over the years, but still provides both an income and a rewarding way of life. For Angus, being part of an ongoing family story on this particular piece of land is central to his identity and wellbeing.

OPPOSITE
Angus and family on the front porch at Clifton. Left to right, standing: Tom, Lucia, Francesca, Abby and Barbara; seated: Angus and Dinah with dogs Rudi and Kate.

As I walk out the kitchen door at seven each morning – earlier if we have a big day on – to take the little dogs Cliff and Kate for a walk, the day takes on a dimension that is new and unique to that day, and yet comfortably the same every day. The sea is always there. The view across the bay to Napier and around to Mahia, or along the cliffs to Black Reef, is always there. The café is always there. The old red woolshed and the old station buildings tucked under the hill are still there. The dogs barking in their kennels are still there. The cheeky pūkeko in the woolshed paddock are always there. As I reach down to pick up the morning paper, I look up the long drive lined with the Moreton Bay fig trees that my father planted, and I see the wood pigeons swooping low and hear the tūī gorging themselves in the giant gums beside Tom's house. This is the beginning of my day come rain or shine, and as I walk back up the drive I lose myself in a reverie so intense that the dogs recognise their moment and set off at a fast deaf run into the hills for a day of rabbit hunting, followed by my curses that once again I've let them get the better of me.

I meet Tom at eight – unless we are doing an early-morning muster – usually at his house now so I can see Francesca, my adorable new blue-eyed granddaughter, and the seventh generation of Gordons at Clifton. Eventually I leave her in the capable hands of her doting mother, and Tom and I head off. Getting into my Can-Am side-by-side, we go down and let off our five sheepdogs, Storm, Grizz, Bounce, Tink and Ruff. After they've all relieved themselves on the same piece of long grass, my two, Storm and Grizz, leap on the back of the Can-Am; Tom's jump onto the back of his four-wheeler.

Off we go through the cutting in the hill, alongside the river, and up the hill to the plateau country we call the Cultivation. Going past the new woolshed and yards, we drop down into the amphitheatre known as the Basin, where the river has carved a circular cliff for itself. Climbing out of another gorge, we come to Round Hill, at the top of which are the pine trees my grandfather Frank planted. In this place, with a view across the wide expanse of the bay, my father John's ashes were scattered. Then on we drive, round the base of this hill, into the paddock we call the Hermit. Travelling alongside the wooded gorge known as Pigeon Gully, we eventually come to the Shallow Creek yards.

This will be our base for the day after we've mustered the cows and calves out of the steep paddock known as Deep Creek. At the back boundary with Taurapa, perched on a razorback ridge above the Maraetotara Falls, we begin pushing the cattle down the river past the rapids. The kōwhai are in spectacular bloom this year. The cows form a long line along the narrow track that takes them past the cabbage-tree grove to the end of the paddock before they begin the long, slow climb up into the Bluffs paddock. By the time they reach the yards, some of the cows with younger calves are getting cranky, so we yard them and then make ourselves a cup of tea.

We begin to draft the cows off the calves in readiness for marking and castrating the calves. Tom's shins and toes will be the worse for wear at the end of the day after he has been stood on and kicked by the frisky little critters. But we return home well satisfied with our day's work, if exhausted.

Some of the happiest times of my farming life have been working with my son. In 2012, he and I formed a farming company called Gordon Farming Limited, and we've enjoyed working together ever since. I've always had a great sense of the history and the beauty of Clifton. My whole working life has been with the one aim of making sure that I can pass the place on to my children in as good, if not better, condition than I received it.

I consider that we are custodians only, and have a great privilege in being a part of such a wonderful environment. With this in mind, I have had to meet the challenges that farming threw at us in the early 1980s. With three massive droughts and plunging commodity prices, we had to change direction away from a complete reliance on, firstly, the wool and then the meat that had been the staple earners of this property for 130-odd years previously.

By diversifying into cropping and irrigation in the late 1980s, building the café in the late 1990s, renovating some of the old farm buildings such as the shearers quarters and old cottage into rental properties, and starting a tourist attraction in the old historic woolshed, we've managed to carry on. We've also changed the emphasis of the farm away from its weaknesses, which are summer-related, to its autumn and spring strengths. By fattening lambs, then at a premium, we have managed to create a more stable and secure environment, which I hope Tom and Lucia will be able to build on. Already they have other plans for the place, such as high-end camping called 'glamping' on spectacular sites around the farm; taking the shearing tourism to the Lodge on Cape Kidnappers Station, and renting some of our land for orcharding and organic cropping ventures.

Looking back on my career, there have been a great many hurdles to overcome and quite a bit of luck – I've managed to survive a total of four serious accidents in the course of my farming life to date, but miraculously have lived to tell the tale each time. We've also experienced some extreme weather events, from terrible droughts to one slip that seriously threatened to destroy the house itself, and we've watched the impact of continual erosion to the beachfront.

The next generation will face problems and other challenges; one being the huge responsibility of eventually taking on the running of this old and very large house and garden. My wife Dinah has performed this job with great diligence since she was thrust into the role in 1989. At that time, my parents moved to a smaller house on Gordon Road in Te Awanga, and we moved from the very manageable and pretty house where Tom and Lucia now live into this wonderful house, where I'd been brought up. Dinah has always understood the historical significance and responsibilities that come with such a beautiful old place. As with all her predecessors, my mother and grandmother included, the garden has always been one of her passions, and over the years she's changed and expanded the flower beds, the most notable being the round garden at the front and the extra gardens on the west side.

We both feel every confidence in the future management of Clifton, because Tom feels as passionate about the place as I do, and has always loved helping me on the farm since he was a kid. As a result, he has turned into an extremely competent farmer who won't be reliant on others as he can perform all the basic tasks a farmer still has to be able to do. And now he has a wife in Lucia, who also loves the place.

Angus's strong attachment to Clifton and keen interest in its origins prompted him to take some time off from farming to write a history of the Gordon family, *In the Shadow of the Cape,* published in 2004. The research he undertook for that project has been an invaluable resource in writing this book, especially for the early chapters about the founding of the station. In recent years, Clifton and its neighbouring properties have taken on several new, unprecedented roles, in tourism and conservation especially.

The story that unfolds is about the Gordon family, but also about the changes and continuities that have shaped this unique section of rural Hawke's Bay from pre-European times to the present.

CHAPTER ONE
BEGINNINGS

OPPOSITE
This portrait of James Gillespie Gordon, by Major Hopkins, 1876, hangs in the dining room at Clifton.
GORDON FAMILY COLLECTION

The founder of Clifton Station, James Gillespie Gordon, was not, as might be expected, a young farmer keen to make his fortune in the Antipodes. Rather, he was 66 years old, with a venerable white beard, white eyebrows and white hair. He came from an old and distinguished Scottish family, and had spent his working life as a successful merchant in the Indian city of Benares (now Varanasi). He'd also managed a large jute plant in India owned by his in-laws, the wealthy Don family of Forfar in Scotland. Upon retiring, he moved back to Forfar with his wife, Elizabeth, who died not long after. He then received unwelcome news of the bank crash in Calcutta following the Indian Mutiny of 1857. This crash dramatically depleted his assets. Instead of accepting this philosophically, he embarked on an enterprising scheme to rebuild the family fortunes.

The solution was simple. He and his two adult sons would travel to the far side of the world and become pastoralists. The adventurousness of this plan – with all its uncertainties and various practical and logistical requirements – speaks volumes about James's determination and energy. His scheme seems especially audacious given that neither he nor his sons had any experience farming sheep.

In the early 1860s, James incrementally purchased 13,000 acres (5260 hectares) on Cape Kidnappers peninsula at the southern tip of Hawke's Bay. This wild, rugged and isolated block of land could hardly have contrasted more sharply with the crowded bustle of India. The Maraetotara River – the block's inland boundary for some 6 miles (10 kilometres) – provided a fresh water source, which was a definite advantage given Hawke's Bay's frequent droughts. Some flat, grassy coastal land east of that river, being bounded by the sea and hills, required no fencing and presented few problems. But the rest of the station's broken, gorgy, spectacular terrain would have challenged even the most experienced sheep farmer. Miles of majestic cliffs extended along the northern face of the peninsula; golden beaches and dunes lined the south-east coast; inland, steep hills, dry riverbeds and precipitous wooded gorges seemed to defy access. Out toward the Cape headland, there was more open, rolling country, with some large hills rising along the east coast.

Even today, the peninsula, although only a 20-minute drive south of the city of Napier, seems a remote, primal landscape. In the mid-nineteenth century, before roads and telephones, the sheer scale and loneliness of the property must have been overwhelming.

When James purchased the land on Cape Kidnappers, it was empty and unpeopled. But it had a long history of human habitation: before Māori sold it to the Crown in 1855, they had lived there for some 500–700 years. Riding over his property, James would have seen evidence of their ancient culture: old pā (fortress) sites dotted the rugged hills and promontories, while the dunes along the south-east coast contained numerous middens. Moreover, many place names on the station and in the surrounding neighbourhood had originated during pre-European times. These names are still in use to this day, while various traditional stories about the origins and special features of Cape Kidnappers have been passed down orally from generation to generation by local iwi (tribes).

MĀORI PLACE NAMES AND TRADITIONAL STORIES

The Māori name for Cape Kidnappers peninsula is Te Matau-a-Māui, or 'the hook of Māui'. According to Māori legend, the headland is a special place, linked to the very origins of New Zealand. The story goes that the legendary Polynesian hero Māui wanted to go fishing with his older brothers, but they refused to take him. So he hid in their boat, only emerging once out at sea. Upon reaching the deepest part of the ocean, he cast a magic fishhook made from an ancestral jawbone, which sank deeper and deeper until it caught on the home of

Tonganui, grandson of Tangaroa, god of the sea. Feeling a powerful tug on his line, Māui realised this was no ordinary haul. Straining and pulling, he eventually landed Te Ika a Māui (the fish of Māui) or the North Island of Aotearoa/New Zealand. The peaked rocks at the end of the Cape Kidnappers headland are the tips of Māui's magic hook: the sacred jawbone used to fish up the North Island was left to form what is now known as Hawke's Bay.

The original Māori inhabitants of Te Matau-a-Māui lived mainly on the coast and along rivers and waterways inland. One of the earliest, Whatonga, was one of three rangatira (chiefs) who journeyed from Hawaiki to Aotearoa aboard the *Kurahaupō* waka and built a house called Heretaunga near Te Matau-a-Māui. The name Heretaunga, now associated primarily with the plains, originally applied to the entire Hawke's Bay region and the bay. 'Here' means to tie and 'taunga' (when applied to a canoe) to come to rest. Tribes from outside the region referred to 'Heretaunga-haukū-nui' – Heretaunga of the heavy dew. This name paid tribute to the region's enviable natural resources: woods filled with plump edible birds, swamps teeming with eels, and abundant seafood or 'kaimoana'.

ABOVE
Cape Kidnappers headland.

In the early sixteenth century, Ngāti Kahungunu began to settle in Te Matau-a-Māui and throughout Heretaunga. Today this iwi is the third largest tribal group in New Zealand, with territory stretching from Māhia to Cape Palliser. Kahungunu, the tribe's handsome, charismatic founder, originally lived around Tūranga (Gisborne), but after conflict among factions, his great grandson, Taraia, led his people south into Heretaunga. This process of resettlement was marked both by conquest (raupatu) and by diplomacy and inter-marriage with the original tribes in the area.

Many Māori place names on Clifton Station and in its vicinity refer to natural resources or topographical features.

The Ngāti Hawea hapū (descended from Kahungunu) were prominent at Te Matau-a-Māui, as were Ngāti Kurukuru of Te Whatuiapiti, an ancient tribe whose members inter-married with Kahungunu but retained a distinct identity. These groups moved about, taking advantage of seasonal resources. They caught seafood from foreshore reefs and deep-sea fishing areas, cultivated kumara, yams and taro on sheltered alluvial flats, and lived in kāinga (villages) nearby.

Many Māori place names on Clifton Station and in its vicinity refer to natural resources or topographical features. Te Awanga is now the site of a thriving village. Originally the name referred not to the flat by the river mouth but to a pā on Karaka Hill – the site where the Summerlee homestead was later built. The flat gets its name from a species of flax called Awanga, which has white streaks in the leaf and grew abundantly in the area. The pā originally belonged to the Kahungunu rangatira Hawea, who, after being wounded in a skirmish between Omāhu and Waiōhiki, withdrew there, biding his time until he could avenge his injury. The earthworks located across The Gap from Te Awanga pā, which are still visible, belonged to another ancient pā called Te Wheturariki.

Just south of the Cape, Puapua, a rocky platform (known to Pākehā as Flat Rock), breaks the beach for a couple of kilometres. Later generations of the Gordon family would enjoy camping and

OPPOSITE TOP
Haupouri sand dunes with Mataurau hills and the point at Whakapau in the distance. Ranga Ika is around the point.

OPPOSITE BOTTOM
The Hill family bach at Cape Kidnappers photographed by Nina Hill. GIFTED BY MRS HOWARD HILL, COLLECTION OF HAWKE'S BAY MUSEUMS TRUST, RUAWHARU TĀ-Ū-RANGI, 12038

picnics there in summer. South of this, to the next point, there are sandy flats known as Ranga Ika. In the 1840s and 1850s, a whaling station operated from this site. The Ranga Ika beach ends at a high bluff called Whakapau, which means to consume or finish. This name derives from a dark story involving two old chiefs who lived near the end of the ridge, a little apart from the rest of the hapu. They carefully levelled a flat place to attract youngsters to play with their spinning tops. After choosing the 'best-favoured' children, they proceeded to kill them, then lowered the bodies down the cliff and carried them to a secluded spot to feast upon.

The northern end of Ocean Beach was called Matarau or Mataraua. There is a small, fairly well preserved pā at the foot of the hills there, and more pits on the higher terrace. The southern end of the beach was known as Haupouri, which means 'dark wind' or 'wind at night'. Before roads were built, this served as a kind of highway from the Waimarama – Māori followed the beach to Flat Rock, then crossed the hill to the beach behind Black Reef. Taurapa, the name of a hill near the beach, means 'carved stern of the canoe'. The name Taurapa was used for the portion of Clifton Station carved off for Charlie Gordon in 1895, while the farm given to

BELOW
View of Te Mata Peak seen from Clifton.

Edward Gordon in 1906 was called Haupouri.

According to tribal tradition, two taniwha (water monsters) created the Tukituki River, to the west of Clifton homestead. They lived in a lake in the upper basin of the present river. A boy accidently fell into the lake, and, while struggling to capture him, the warring taniwha formed the Waipawa and Tukituki rivers, which drained and thus 'demolished' (or tukituki'd) the original lake. A pā and kāinga were located at Waipureku, a name that means 'the meeting place of waters', because this was then the joint river mouth of the Tukituki and Ngaruroro rivers.

Te Mata Peak, a spectacular local landmark at the western boundary of the Heretaunga Plains, is visible from the back of Clifton Station. The promontory reaches 399 metres. According to Māori tradition, Te Mata Peak is the prostrate body of Rongokako, grandfather of Kahungunu and ancestor of all Kahungunu iwi. When, in ancient times, coastal Waimarama tribes invaded the Heretaunga Plains, the local people hatched a scheme to get Rongokako to fall in love with Hinerakau, daughter of a Pakipaki chief. They made Hinerakau insist that Rongokako perform many feats to prove his love. His last task was to bite his way through the hills between the

coast and the plains so people could come and go with greater ease. He choked on the earth of Te Mata Peak, however, and his half-accomplished work can be seen today in The Gap or Pari Kārangaranga (echoing cliffs). The outline of Rongokako's body forms the skyline, with his head to the south and his feet to the north. European settlers also thought the hills resembled a man lying down and called him the 'Sleeping Giant'. The Peak was known as Te Mata O Rongokako or 'The Face of Rongokako', which has been shortened to Te Mata Peak over time.

THE NAMING OF CAPE KIDNAPPERS

In 1769, Te Matau-a-Māui received a new European name: Cape Kidnappers. As with so many other New Zealand place names, Captain James Cook bestowed it on his first voyage of discovery aboard *Endeavour*. His journal entry of 15 October 1769 describes the dramatic events that resulted in this unusual name:

> At 8 am being a breast of the sw Point of the Bay, some fishing boats came off to us, and sold us some stinking fish [dried shark]; however it was such as the[y] had, and we were glad to enter into traffick with them upon any terms. These people behaved at first very well, until a large arm'd boat wherein were 22 Men, came along side.

OPPOSITE
Black Reef
looking towards
the Cape.

In the ensuing exchange, Cook believed he had traded a piece of red cloth for a 'black skin, something like a bear skin' (probably a dog-skin cloak), but to his indignation did not receive it. The canoes and fishing boats then put off but soon returned. One of the fishing boats came alongside offering more fish, then:

> *The Indian boy Tiata, Tupia's servent being over the side, they seized hold of him, pulled him into the boat and endeavour'd to carry him off, this obliged us to fire upon them which gave the Boy an opportunity to jump over board and we brought the Ship too, lower'd a boat into the Water and took him up unhurt. Two or three paid for this daring attempt with the loss of their lives and many more would have suffered had it [not] been for fear of killing the boy. This affair occasion'd my giving this point of Land the name of Cape Kidnappers . . .*

Upon recovering, the boy Tiata (often spelled Tayeto) brought a fish for Tupaia, Cook's Tahitian translator, to offer his god in thanks for

BELOW
Looking back at Cape Kidnappers.

this fortunate escape. Tupaia approved the gesture, and advised Tiata to throw it into the sea.

The motivations behind this attempted abduction remain obscure to this day. Writing in his journal in 1851, the Anglican missionary William Colenso recorded that some Waimarama Māori, descendants of individuals involved in the affray, told him that Tupaia had warned their fathers not to approach the ship, saying 'Mai, mate koe' (Here, thou wilt be killed). Their priests and chiefs ignored this warning, however, believing the newcomers to be Hawaiians armed only with stalks of flax and reeds.

Some Māori have perceived the events of 17 October 1769 as a rescue attempt. The *Evening Post* of 30 December 1995, for example, reported that according to Te Reo Areare, a coalition of Māori education groups: 'Māori believed their ancestors thought the Tahitian was being held by Captain Cook's crew, and wanted to free him. The accusation of kidnapping was inaccurate.' Whatever the reason behind the unfortunate incident, it introduced Māori to the lethal power of firearms and resulted in two deaths.

ABOVE
Joseph Rhodes's sketch of Waimarama with Cape Kidnappers in the distance, c. 1850s.
ALEXANDER TURNBULL LIBRARY, WELLINGTON, NZ: A-159-034

TRADERS AND WHALERS

Before the Gordons arrived in the early 1860s, the lands and the waters surrounding what would later become Clifton Station were the scene of much energetic commerce and trade. By the 1840s, the Māori residents of Cape Kidnappers peninsula had been joined by a number of shore-based whalers. Between 1844 and 1848, a whaling station operated on the south-east coast of the Cape at Ranga Ika. (This land, formerly part of Clifton Station, now forms part of Cape Kidnappers Station.) European whalers were not new to the area: they had first visited Hawke's Bay in 1796, but stayed offshore. In ensuing decades, mainly British and American whalers hunted sperm whales off the coast, periodically coming ashore in search of fresh water, wood, flax for rope, vegetables and fresh meat to prevent scurvy.

Shore-based whaling, which boomed throughout Hawke's Bay in the 1840s, focused on the black or right whale, which migrated in early winter, along the east coast of the North Island, staying close to the shore. William Morris, a formidably bearded Irishman known to Māori as 'Moreke', owned and ran the whaling operation at Ranga Ika. He paid its patron and landlord, the rangatira Tiakitai from Waimarama, a fee of £5 per annum for whaling, fishing, and occupation rights. Tiakitai, known to the European whaling community as 'Jacky Tie', owned his own whaleboat, which he used both for whaling and trading. He died when the boat capsized in rough seas en route to a wedding feast in Māhia in 1847. Thereafter, Morris gave the rangatira Kurupo Te Moananui the annual fee for the station.

In 1844, Ranga Ika had three whaleboats and employed about 20 whalers. These men needed to be strong, fit and courageous. The rocky entrance to the sandy horse-shoe-shaped bay, where the whaleboats were kept, heightened the danger. Any mistake made entering or leaving could have dire consequences. Morris's eldest son, William, later recalled that whalers 'thought nothing of rowing a whale-boat 40 or 50 miles to borrow a tri-pot if there was none available where the dead whale was beached.' Morris Senior, described as 'one of the most fearless men who ever went out', lost an eye in a harpooning accident. He reputedly once spotted a dark object in the water and ordered his brother-in-law, Nepia Tokitahi, to harpoon it. Despite being told that the object in question was a rock, Morris insisted. The rock was subsequently dubbed 'Tokitia'. Friends and relatives teased Morris about the incident for the rest of his life.

> **Morris Senior, described as 'one of the most fearless men who ever went out', lost an eye in a harpooning accident.**

Like many other whalers, Morris eventually branched into trade, running shops in Poverty Bay and Napier. He also leased land near Wairoa for raising sheep, and was engaged part-time in the coastal trade between Hawke's Bay and the Bay of Islands. Most whalers participated in some sort of trading, both during and after their whaling days. Trading and whaling were inextricably linked. To survive, offshore European whalers traded with Māori, while resident whalers often busied themselves in the off-season by trading items such as pigs, fish and flax.

Many shore-based whalers, again like Morris, married local

high-ranking Māori women. Hapū looked upon these unions as a good connection because they created a beneficial alliance in terms of trade. Māori frequently formed the core of many whaling gangs, both hunting and processing the whales. They also actively engaged in coastal trade, with whale oil, whalebone, pigs, flax and corn being the chief trading products of the district. Several entrepreneurial Heretaunga Māori had schooners; others owned their own clinker-built whaleboats in preference to canoes.

The often drunken and rowdy behaviour of whalers soon attracted critics among respectable settler society. By the late 1850s, however, there were fewer badly-behaved whalers to vilify. The whaling trade was petering out due to the scarcity of whales, although it continued into the 1880s on a smaller scale. Whalers who stayed on in the region likely had other sources of income from trading or pastoralism; those with Māori wives were more likely to have the use of hapū land.

By the time James Gillespie Gordon founded Clifton Station in the early 1860s, the whaling station at Ranga Ika had ceased operating. There were doubtless still stories circulating about the whaling among locals, however, and James might well have come across some tangible evidence of the trade.

Today, visitors to Clifton can still see two picturesque relics of the industry. Local farmers Michael Neilson and Bill Shaw dug three tri-pots out of the sand dunes during the 1970s. After Bill restored them, Angus Gordon purchased two and set them on either side of the Clifton Café entrance as an interesting decorative feature linked to the Cape's whaling heritage.

One important legacy of whaling and trading was the idea among Māori that having Europeans in their midst increased both tribal mana and prosperity. This in turn influenced the view that selling land to the Crown would lift tribal fortunes, by drawing in more European settlers and increasing opportunities for trade. James Gillespie Gordon and other aspiring pastoralists benefited from this notion, because it helped to spur Māori land sales in Te Matau-a-Māui and elsewhere. The circumstances that led to those early land sales, and the subsequent impact of land sales on race relations, directly influenced the history of the station later in the 1860s.

OPPOSITE
Tri-pots at Clifton Café.

The Whaler and the Missionary

Around the time shore-based whalers began hunting off the south-east coast of Cape Kidnappers, Christian missionaries arrived in Hawke's Bay. In 1844 the region acquired its own resident missionary, William Colenso. He and his wife, Elizabeth, lived in a cottage at Waitangi, near the mouth of the Tukituki River. Unfortunately for the Colensos, this highly problematic site regularly flooded in winter and suffered swamp-like pestilence in summer.

Colenso established a small school for his flock, and converted some prominent local rangatira to Christianity. By the late 1840s and early 1850s, he was voicing concern about

ABOVE
W. Morris Wholesale and Retail Store in Waghorne Street, Ahuriri, c. 1870s–80s.
GIFTED BY MRS ROWE, COLLECTION OF HAWKE'S BAY MUSEUMS TRUST, RUAWHARU TĀ-Ū-RANGI, 2125

the pace and scale of land sales, repeatedly urging chiefs to set aside reserves for future generations. His opposition to Māori selling their land, combined with an at times inflexible personality, did not win him many friends among the fledgling Hawke's Bay Pākehā community. He did, however, make one lasting friend among locals: William Morris, the master whaler who ran the Ranga Ika station. After Morris left the district, the pair corresponded frequently. In one 1852 letter, Colenso associated the view of the Cape from his cottage with memories of his old neighbour:

> *I scarcely ever walk in my verandah and look toward the Cape but I think of you. That Cape and yourself somehow seem as if linked in my mind. Perhaps it is owing to you being our nearest white neighbour during the first years of your residence there.*
>
> *I had heard you are doing well, having some luck in the sperm whale way . . . Not that I think you will ever become rich, this is, as the term is generally used: yet a contented mind is riches and to this I do not think you are a stranger . . .*

In the same letter, Colenso expressed some disapproval about rumours that Morris had opened a public house: 'I would rather you follow anything else than grog-selling', and also expressed concern about what would happen to Māori if they persisted in selling land:

> *I believe the Natives act much as children with a box of gingerbread, a bit today, then a bit tomorrow with the usual 'heoi ano', what then . . .*

THE RHODES BROTHERS AND THE CAPE KIDNAPPERS RUN

A few years before Colenso arrived in Hawke's Bay, Captain William Barnard Rhodes audaciously attempted to purchase almost all of the land in the region. His attempt, though ultimately unsuccessful, had an indirect influence on James Gillespie Gordon's later purchase of Clifton Station.

In 1839, Rhodes, an ambitious English-born sea captain, arrived in New Zealand aboard the *Eleanor*. Working in partnership with the Sydney firm Cooper and Holt, he began buying land from Māori and establishing trading agents on both islands. In December 1839, he built a trading post at Waipureku and set up a man called Simmons to run it. There Māori traded dressed flax and pork, and possibly maize and potatoes in season, for European goods such as sugar and blankets. (Simmons was apparently not a hit among his customers, as they later razed his store and goods.) Rhodes meanwhile busily established more trading posts at Ahuriri, Mahia and Wairoa.

Writing back to his Sydney partners in January, he informed them proudly:

My last purchase is described as follows: All that tract of land in the Northern Island of New Zealand commencing at Cape Turnagain, thence continuing the line of coast to the north around Cape Kidnapper to a White Cliff, bounded on the east by the sea and partly by Hawke's Bay, extending into the interior, or westward, 30 miles, and parallel with the coast. Reserving 1/10 for the use of the natives and estimated at 1,401,600 acres for about £150. I want one man's signature yet to this deed. This immense tract is very valuable.

Captain Rhodes never did obtain the missing signature, and his various acquisitions (totalling 1,575,411.5 acres – almost 640,000 hectares – in both islands) were disallowed following the signing of the Treaty of Waitangi in 1840. He did, however, receive from the Land Claims Commissioner 100,000 acres (40,000 hectares) at Rissington and a 4500-acre (1800-hectare) block on the south side of

ABOVE
Joseph Rhodes's Clive Grange sheep station, 1860s.
ALEXANDER TURNBULL LIBRARY, WELLINGTON, NZ: PA1-Q-193-019-1

the mouth of the Tukituki River, which is believed to be the origin of the Clive Grange Estate, west of Clifton Station. He also received the Waipureku trading post as compensation for the Hawke's Bay purchase, and in 1880, his former business, Rhodes, Cooper and Holt, received a scrip certificate of £2560.

WB Rhodes, who eventually became a pillar of Wellington society, never lived at Clive Grange Station himself. Because he had several properties, he encouraged his many brothers to move to New Zealand and run them in partnership with him. His youngest brother, Joseph, took up the Clive Grange property in 1855, and also procured a further 200 acres (80 hectares) at Waipureku for £130 from the chief Te Moananui. In 1859–60 Joseph Rhodes bought some 2036 acres (800 hectares) of Te Matau-a-Māui from the Crown, including the Cape itself. This land, Crown Granted in 1861 and used to farm sheep, was known as the Kidnappers Run, and would later form part of Clifton Station.

Joseph Rhodes, a successful pastoralist, became a prominent public figure in Hawke's Bay, spearheading the push for the region to become a separate province in 1858, and playing an active role on the

Provincial Council. In 1855, he also commissioned surveyor Henry Tiffen to lay out a township made up of 600 quarter-acre sections, a short distance from the Māori village at Waipureku on the north bank of the Tukituki. He named the town Clive, and it was situated in the area now known as East Clive. Settlement remained slow, however, as the site was susceptible to floods. Nevertheless, by the 1850s and 1860s, Clive boasted several stores, a bakery, two hotels, a post office, a public school, a police station, a blacksmith, and a ferry service over the Tukituki.

LAND SALES AND A BITTER RIVALRY

A few months after Captain WB Rhodes's attempted purchase, on 23 June 1840, HMS *Herald* anchored opposite the Tukituki River mouth. Governor Hobson had delegated those on board to obtain Māori signatures to the Treaty of Waitangi.

Under the Treaty, European settlers were not allowed to enter into land sales or lease agreements with Māori. Nevertheless, unauthorised run-holders continued to deal directly with Māori. For example, Hawke's Bay's first pastoralists, James Northwood and Henry Tiffen, obtained some 50,000 acres (20,000 hectares) at Pourere and Makere, and by 1849 boasted a flock of some 3000 sheep. Alarmed at illegal leasing on this scale, the government appointed a capable young Scot, Donald McLean, as Land Commissioner for Hawke's Bay. He arrived in December 1850 and set about vigorously prosecuting those with extra-legal leases and pressing Māori to sell the freehold. McLean greatly admired the area, quickly perceiving its potential for pastoralism. Writing to his superiors in December 1850, he enthused:

> *It is essentially necessary that the utmost expedition be used to acquire this splendid district, which is peculiarly adapted for sheep grazing, and which would be readily taken up by the Wairarapa settlers, whose flocks are increasing so rapidly that they must shortly have an outlet for them.*

Hawke's Bay chiefs eagerly sold land to the Crown because they still believed European neighbours would ensure trade and prosperity. But debt was another important factor spurring sales: many heavily indebted rangatira needed sale money to pay off creditors. Rivalry over a rangatira's right to sell, a reflection of mana and pre-eminence, also played a part in prompting sales, as did McLean's considerable diplomatic skill and powers of persuasion.

The chief Te Hapuku, a leading land seller in Hawke's Bay, characteristically often entered into sale negotiations with the Crown without telling other interested parties. McLean, despite being informed by Colenso that there were other local rangatira of mana he should consult, seems to have consciously decided to deal as much as possible with Te Hapuku. This tactic worked well. Early in 1851 he acquired the Waipukurau, Ahuriri and Mohaka blocks (some 255,000 hectares) for the Crown. Although Te Moananui participated in the sale of Waipukurau and Ahuriri, he and other local chiefs resented McLean's apparent belief that Te Hapuku was the leading chief of Heretaunga. As rivalry between Te Hapuku and Te Moananui escalated, land sales forged ahead.

THE SALE OF TE MATAU-A-MĀUI: SECOND THOUGHTS

On 23 March 1855, Te Moananui, by then indisputably the paramount rangatira in Te Matau-a-Māui, sold the 30,000-acre (12,000 hectare) Te Matau-a-Māui block to the Crown for £2000, reserving a 300-acre (120-hectare) piece of land at Ranga Ika for Māori. McLean, as Land Commissioner, signed the deed, as did Te Moananui and 32 others.

The following year, Te Moananui attended the historic meeting at Poukawa at which it was proposed to create a Māori King. He left the meeting believing land sales should stop. On the pretext that the Crown had not paid him for some land in the Ruahine Range, he refused for a time to accept the second instalment of the payment for Te Matau-a-Māui, hoping to force the return of some of that land. A number of his people, also unhappy with the loss of Te Matau-a-Māui, supported this stance. But in the end the sale proceeded. The Crown paid the final £1000 in July 1857. Despite his support for the King movement, Te Moananui needed the money from the sale to settle debts. He later entered into further land sales to try to clear them.

In August 1857, rivalry between Te Hapuku and Te Moananui erupted into war. Te Moananui had given Te Hapuku the right to take firewood at Pakiaka, a piece of bush near Clive. Te Hapuku began cutting down trees, then announced his intention to build a new pā there to defend his rights. Three separate battles ensued, all of which Te Moananui won, resulting in 14 deaths and many wounded. Donald McLean eventually persuaded his old friend Te Hapuku to accept Te Moananui's requirement to move inland to Te Hauke. By this stage, local Europeans were seriously alarmed. Troops were called in for protection in February 1858. Te Hapuku left for his new home in March, burning down Whataku pā as he left. By October 1858, the government had stationed 160 soldiers in Napier to help quell local fears.

Like the rest of the country, race relations in Hawke's Bay grew increasingly strained. Te Moananui still supported the Māori King, having been appointed kāwana (governor) of the Heretaunga region by King Tāwhiao. The King movement, which did not recognise British sovereignty, might have taken hold in Hawke's Bay had more local rangatira agreed with its tenets. But Karaitiana Takamoana, Te Moananui's successor as paramount chief, never became a Kingite. Nevertheless, tensions remained high. In 1861 Cooper recommended halting further land sales in the area and McLean agreed. In the same year, Te Moananui passed away. His fears about the repercussions of land sales had proved well founded. As a result of so much land loss, the balance of power between Māori and settlers altered irrevocably. By this time, the Crown had purchased nearly 2 million acres (800,000 hectares) in northern and central Hawke's Bay at an average price of two shillings an acre – the equivalent of about $11 in modern money. In the course of the 1850s and early 1860s, it sold large blocks of this land, at five shillings per acre for pastoral and 10 shillings for agricultural.

OPPOSITE
Portrait of Te Hapuku, taken by Samuel Carnell in the 1870s. Te Hapuku was a brilliant orator with a great knowledge of Māori tradition. Although he rejected Christianity, he allowed Christian missionaries to teach his children, and was the prime instigator of gifting lands to the missionaries for the establishment of Te Aute College in 1854.
ALEXANDER TURNBULL LIBRARY, WELLINGTON, NZ: 1/4-022221-G

SHEEP FARMING PREVAILS

Within a relatively short timeframe, sheep farming prevailed over all other forms of agriculture. By 1856, Hawke's Bay boasted approximately 700,000 acres (283,000 hectares) of land in pastoral production. Wool exports, primarily to Britain, were worth £20,000 annually, while the station owners who enabled this trade numbered only 30-some. On 14 December 1861, the *Hawke's Bay Herald* complained that 'the land of the whole Province passes into the hands of a few proprietors, to be used in unimproved state as sheep walks'.

Owners of large stations, men such as John Davies Ormond and Joseph Rhodes, soon dominated provincial government. The returns on their runs gave them the means to purchase more land, set up towns, establish industries and get involved in a range of ventures from sawmilling to goldmining to land speculation. They resided in gracious homes with well-tended grounds, generally set the tone of local society, and occupied its top rung. A considerable number of Hawke's Bay's early pastoralists came from Scotland: men such as Donald McLean, the brothers Henry and T Purvis Russell, JG Kinross, Hugh Campbell and Alexander McHardy. Although James Gillespie Gordon was far from being the only enterprising Scot to take up pastoralism in Hawke's Bay, few of his compatriots would have done so at such an advanced age. Fortunately, his late-in-life gamble paid off, but not before presenting a series of challenges, great and small.

CHAPTER TWO
FOUNDING CLIFTON

James Gillespie Gordon's decision to start a new life as a sheep farmer in New Zealand would not have been taken lightly. The colony could hardly have been more geographically remote: just getting there was a major undertaking. According to family lore, James sailed to New Zealand from India in his own schooner in 1859. Whether travelling in a boat of his own or as a passenger on someone else's vessel, the journey was long and potentially dangerous. Frightening storms could blow up at any time, fire might break out, or illness set in; even if these potential perils did not eventuate, the voyage involved considerable discomfort and monotonous tedium. From a practical perspective, there was a great deal to organise before embarking. As well as bringing all of the provisions needed for the journey, James had to think about the future and how he and his sons would live in their new country. Accordingly he also transported the prefabricated makings of a future homestead, some handsome handcrafted Indian teak furniture, one capacious cast-iron bath and a team of white Indian army mules (originally imported from Arabia), from India to the Antipodes.

Upon arriving in New Zealand in 1859, James lived for a time in Bow Cottage, Nelson; a 'very substantial and newly-arranged dwelling house', with garden, paddock, and one and a quarter acres. He had managed to persuade his sons Thomas Edward and William Cracroft to leave their military careers – both were British Army cavalry captains in India – and join him in his pastoralist adventure. Thomas, who was married, had various matters to attend to before he could emigrate, but William, who was single, arrived in Nelson on the *Mataoka* in September 1859. Leaving everything he knew and loved,

from friends and family to a successful career in the army, for an extremely remote unknown country and an untried occupation must have been a formidable prospect for the young ex-military man.

James and William did not remain in Nelson long. By January 1861, they were on Joseph Rhodes's Kidnappers Run. In February of that year they purchased 1100 acres (445 hectares) from Rhodes, and a year later, in 1862, bought 6400 adjoining acres (2590 hectares) from the Crown. Within a few years they acquired more land from Rhodes and others, until the station comprised some 13,000 acres (5260 hectares), including the Cape itself.

NAMING, EXPLORING AND SETTLING IN

ABOVE
Plan of the Kidnapper Estate, 1861.
GORDON FAMILY COLLECTION

Upon arrival, James and William set up tents at the flat site where they intended to build a homestead. The coastal lands surrounding this spot had some dry grass, as Joseph Rhodes had run sheep there for several years. From this base, father and son then spent a considerable time riding out over the peninsula, trying to become more familiar with the very unfamiliar landscape. The flora and fauna proved dramatically different from anything they had previously encountered. The forests were dense with mysterious native trees such as karaka and tītoki, rewarewa or honeysuckle, fine-leafed kōwhai that burst into brilliant yellow flowers in spring, grey shrub-like mānuka and the taller, darker kānuka, with its dark pink flowers. Even the bird species were unfamiliar. Shiny black tūī sported white ruffs that made them look like parsons. James and William dubbed one formidable gorge traversing the property for some two miles Pigeon Gully because it teemed with fat native wood pigeons or kererū.

Faced with this exotic environment, James opted to give the station a familiar name, one that reflected his British and Indian heritage. Clifton was the name of a popular beach resort for the English not far from Karachi, and also of the school he attended as a boy in England. The Indian aspect fitted in with other place names in the region, such as Napier, Clive, Meeanee and Scinde Island.

Faced with this exotic environment, James opted to give the station a familiar name, one that reflected his British and Indian heritage.

Although Clifton had a good source of water in the Maraetotara River, James wondered if there was another water source close to the chosen homestead site. One of the men he had hired to work as a carpenter on the house spotted a green area halfway up the hill. They investigated there and, to everyone's gratification, found a steady flow of water coming out of the ground. Exploring further, they discovered a seam running parallel to this, where there were other springs. From here they could dig pools to collect water and, later, lay pipes down to the house site. In the meantime, the mules could carry it down in containers. James had brought tanks for collecting rainwater off the roof of the new house once it was built. Things were fitting into place nicely. Moreover, many of the hills appeared to be covered with a type

of bracken, interspersed with some sort of native grasses. This bracken could be burnt off and the grasses, when combined with introduced species, would hopefully thrive.

On subsequent exploratory rides, James and William discovered long fingers of plateau land dissected by gorges, with the cover across the hills a mixture of green fern on the southern side and brown grass along the northern and exposed slopes. Upon rounding the Cape, they saw elegant gannets diving and swooping, a dazzling display of white, gold and black. They also saw many tracks made by wild pigs. Alarmingly, several of these formidable beasts careened in front of them. The 'Captain Cookers' – descended from pigs Captain Cook had released into the wild – might be tasty, but they posed a real threat to any future stock. Fortunately, William enjoyed shooting them.

> **Upon rounding the Cape, they saw elegant gannets diving and swooping, a dazzling display of white, gold and black.**

They found they could bring the stock down from Porpoise Gully, which came down behind Black Reef, and had a continuous supply of fresh water from springs further back. This would give them good access to all the Cape country. They then found they could, when the tide was out, follow the shoreline beneath the cliffs back to the Clifton homestead site. This ride was easy and quick, and would be a perfect stock route if they accurately calculated the tides.

James's next priority, building a house, was less

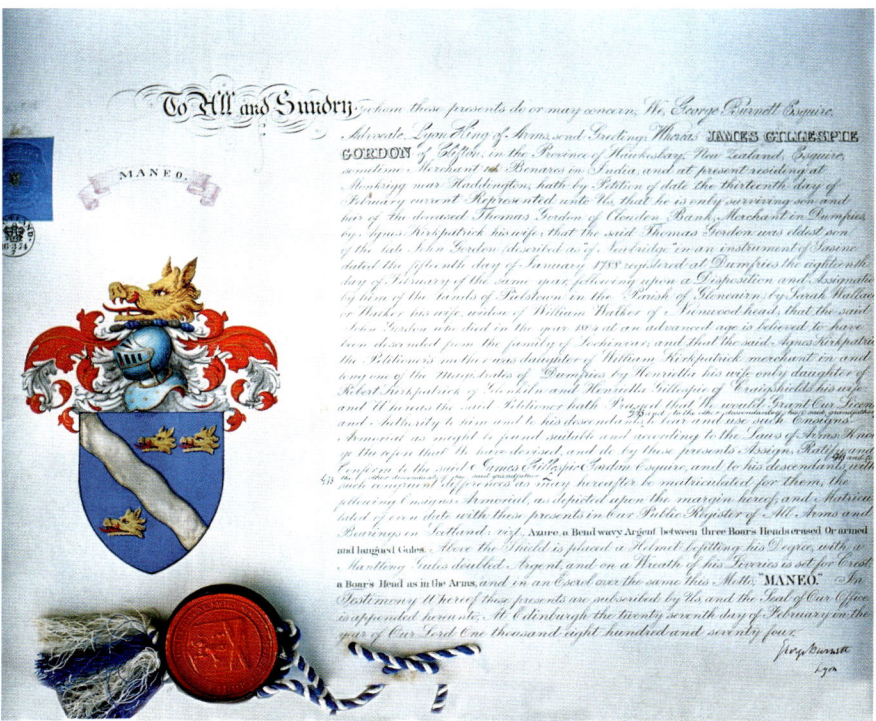

ABOVE
In 1874 James Gillespie Gordon became the first New Zealander to be granted a coat of arms by the Senior Herald in Scotland. The inclusion of a boar's head in the coat of arms, along with the latin motto 'Maneo', (I endure/remain) was perhaps an intentional reference to Clifton, where wild pigs posed a threat to stock during the station's early years.
GORDON FAMILY COLLECTION

daunting than it might have been, because all of the necessary supplies – from prefabricated timbers to roof shingles to furniture – had made the long ship's journey from India to New Zealand. Although bringing this sort of ready-made accommodation was not uncommon among wealthier segments of the settler population, the materials usually derived from Britain or Australia rather than India. Neatly packed and labelled, the makings of the Gordons' future house were stacked ashore, waiting to be assembled. (The cast-iron bath suffered a bit of cosmetic damage, having been kicked by one of the mules, but was still perfectly serviceable.)

The new homestead did not take long to erect. Nestled against the hills on flat land some 120 metres from the beach, it was a charming, comfortable residence with stunning views of the sea and Cape. Its simple, pleasing design – recognisably Indian in origin – included a central front structure with two dormer windows, and two symmetrical steepled rooms at each end. A sweeping verandah extended across the front and along the sides of the house. Three long buildings located immediately behind housed separate servants' quarters, an office, laundry, scullery and extra guest-bedrooms.

ABOVE
This intricately carved sideboard, brought from India by James Gillespie Gordon, is in the front hall of the Clifton homestead.

James purchased two Norfolk pines at Port Ahuriri and planted them about 35 metres from each side of the house, having been informed, correctly as it turned out, that they would flourish in stony soil.

The next step was to buy sheep. James instructed William to burn off some of the bracken in readiness to oversow grass when the rains came, and to oversee the final stages of completing the homestead. He then sailed for Sydney, where he bought some pure-bred Merino ewes and rams – an obvious choice for the dry Hawke's Bay country – and also hired two Scottish shepherds, who returned with him to work on Clifton. These men later helped to design a shearing shed based on Scottish models, with a mezzanine floor for wool storage and a block-and-pulley system to get the wool bales up. Upon returning to Ahuriri, James purchased more sheep as well as horses. By the end of 1861 the station had 8032 sheep, half of which were ewes.

The station made a promising start. Everything seemed to augur well. After the initial challenges of getting established, James and William were comfortably ensconced in a well-furnished home, with domestic servants and shepherds to help in their new undertaking, and the heartening sight of sheep browsing contentedly on the flats.

Less positively, there was the threat that weather, drought especially, could bring to their plans, to say nothing of an outbreak of disease. Moreover it seemed that Donald McLean's assurances about hard-working, placidly obliging local Māori masked a much more complex, troubled reality.

At the same time, James and William could take heart in the fact that Hawke's Bay pastoralists were flourishing, enjoying unrivalled political influence and social prestige. Owners of neighbouring estates offered the Gordons hospitality and advice, and nearby towns and villages had pubs and shops. Admittedly, there were three rivers and two streams to cross between Napier and Clifton and no bridges, so the process of getting into town by land was often fraught or even impossible. The Tukituki River in particular blighted many proposed journeys to Napier. If it rose too high, then the 13-kilometre return journey on horseback was a tiring waste of time and energy. Nevertheless, although the lack of bridges remained problematic, roads were slowly starting to be built throughout Hawke's Bay, and the services, facilities and entertainments on offer in various local communities were also beginning to develop and grow.

TOWNS AND TRANSPORT

Pastoralism created a pressing need for more and better roads. Early exporters and importers were totally dependent on water transport by sea or through swamp, rivers and lagoons; their plans and profits frequently stymied by rising waters or unscrupulous ferry operators. The wool clip from various inland stations was punted down the Tukituki and loaded onto vessels in the bay at Waipureku by way of a whale- or surf-boat: the 4-ton *Sailors' Pride* plied between Waipureku and Napier. Lighters and coastal traders brought goods to coastal stations where road access was slow or non-existent.

Between 1863 and 1866, James Gordon, in partnership with S Begg and JG Kinross, owned a 58-ton schooner called *Success*. He used this vessel on a wool run, picking up wool clip from coastal stations and transporting it to Napier. James was also, with other prominent local pastoralists such as Donald McLean and HS Tiffen, a shareholder in the Hawke's Bay Steam Navigation Company,

OPPOSITE TOP
The original homestead in the late nineteenth century.

OPPOSITE BOTTOM
Going on a picnic at Taurapa.
MICHAEL GORDON COLLECTION

set up to purchase a 300-ton steamer for the Napier coastal trade. This acquisition was both necessary and desirable, because, as the company prospectus of 3 January 1863 noted: 'The want of a suitable local steamer has been severely felt for the past eighteen months – flock owners and others having been thereby shut out from the high markets existing both in Otago and Auckland.' By 1864 the company had merged with the New Zealand Steam Navigation Company, which ran seven steamers throughout the country.

Road maintenance proved especially challenging in Hawke's Bay because of the climate, with floods wreaking havoc or long droughts and high winds whipping up dust.

The dependence on water transport lessened very gradually, as the number and quality of roads slowly improved. In the course of the 1860s and 1870s the Hawke's Bay Provincial Council set about organising the construction of several major thoroughfares, including the Te Aute Road and the vital Middle or Napier Road from Napier to Waipukurau, which greatly improved residents' ability to travel by land. Not all roads were freely available; for example, the only road into Taradale from the coast during the 1860s was a tollway via Meeanee, which skirted the swamp to join the main road between Napier and Clive. Tolls were collected at Tareha's Bridge, near Awatoto.

Road maintenance proved especially challenging in Hawke's Bay because of the climate, with floods wreaking havoc or long droughts and high winds whipping up dust. Indignant letters about the appalling state of country roads featured regularly in the local press.

Napier had, by the early 1860s, established itself as the region's leading town. Its advantages were its harbour and the fact that it was the provincial capital. Sheep farming drove the local economy, and Napier was the wool-exporting centre. The wool trade generated a wide range of associated business, from banks to insurance companies, wool-brokers, meat-processing plants, blacksmiths, stock and station agents, general stores and hotels; basically everything needed to support a farming community. The main

ABOVE
View of Napier from Bluff Hill c. 1865–73. Cape Kidnappers is visible in the distance.
VALENTINE & SONS LIMITED, FROM THE ESTATE OF MR CECIL DOUGLAS CORNFORD, COLLECTION OF HAWKE'S BAY MUSEUMS TRUST, RUAWHARU TĀ-Ū-RANGI, 1893

business district was a triangle of flat land south of Scinde Hill. According to Dr Thomas Hitchings, the Provincial Surgeon, the swamps surrounding this area generated 'a variety of noxious and pestilential gases'. Although a watery, seemingly unlikely location for a town, Napier steadily grew and prospered. Total exports rose from an average annual value of £16,499 (of which wool made up £15,591) in the years 1860–64 to £154,941 (of which wool made up £154,429) in 1870–74.

In addition to business and politics, Napier offered various recreational attractions and community facilities. *The Hawke's Bay Herald* commenced in 1857; an Athenaeum and Mechanics' Institute opened in 1859, and a purpose-built hospital in 1860. Sports such as cricket, swimming, rowing, fishing, and boating flourished among all social classes; with rugby a relative latecomer in the 1870s. One of the most important social clubs, the exclusive (male-only) Hawke's Bay Club, founded in 1863, provided pastoralists, leading businessmen and professionals with a comfortable venue in which to enjoy cards, billiards and gossip. This facility, also used for transacting business, helped to recreate a desirable aspect of English town life. Although the annual club fee was relatively high, membership was a definite social asset.

> **Twenty kilometres west of the Cape, East Clive/Waipureku was for a time a flourishing community because of its location at the meeting point of the Ngaruroro and Tukituki rivers.**

Less exclusive hotels and pubs also provided places to socialise and quench one's thirst. Enterprising publicans often set up booths at particular events. For example, at Napier's Race Days, held in early March, a much-anticipated social event extending over two days, usually about half a dozen publicans' booths on-site satisfied the thirsty and boisterous clientele. The *Hawke's Bay Herald* of 3 March 1863 refers to a rain-plagued but still enjoyable Race Day. That evening, the Scinde Masonic Lodge hosted a ball to celebrate its new hall in Tennyson Street. Napier also boasted a growing number of schools and churches. In 1862 James Gillespie Gordon's name featured on a list of subscribers supporting the establishment of a Presbyterian Church School in Napier. Along with other pastoralists, he also served as a trustee of the Napier Savings Bank.

While Napier was the premier Hawke's Bay town, 20 kilometres west of the Cape, East Clive/Waipureku was for a time a flourishing community because of its location at the meeting point of the Ngaruroro and Tukituki rivers. As Gary Baines's recent history of Clive points out, however, with the new main road bypassing the township, a bridge crossing the Ngaruroro from 1867, and the railway opening to the west in the early 1870s, West Clive began to flourish. Following flooding in 1867, the Ngaruroro's course changed, which meant that Waipureku no longer comprised the meeting place of the two rivers.

The Ngaruroro's changed course also ended plans to make Havelock (later Havelock North) a focus of water transport.

Fortunately that village, created in 1860, was located at the junction of six roads. The Provincial Engineer, reporting for the period ending 30 April 1861, noted: 'On the Te Aute Road the traffic has been very considerable . . . it being no unusual occurrence to meet in the course of the day 10, 12, or as many as 15 bullock drays going over it, all heavily laden.' Thirsty drivers called in at the Havelock Hotel, where publican John Bray also served as the town's first postmaster. In 1863 Havelock hosted the first show of the Hawke's Bay Agricultural Society in Mr Danvers' paddock on Napier Road. The *Hawke's Bay Herald* of 21 October described the day as 'quite a gala one', concluding more circumspectly, 'considering this was a first attempt . . . the results on the whole, must be regarded as having been of a very encouraging and promising character'.

Despite the fact that local towns and pastoralism generally enjoyed a 'very encouraging and promising character' by the early 1860s, the life of a Hawke's Bay sheep farmer differed radically from that of a cavalry officer in India. William missed his former occupation dearly, his moods darkened and he showed no sign of warming to his new career. James was doubtless pleased to welcome his younger son to the station.

THOMAS AND JANET ARRIVE

On 1 March 1862, Captain Thomas Edward Gordon and his wife, Janet, arrived in Napier, having spent a month in Wellington waiting for a steamer to take them on the final stage of their journey. During that time, the government asked Thomas, a handsome, imposing-looking military man, if he would raise a volunteer cavalry troop in Napier. He agreed, receiving a commission as Captain of the 'Napier Cavalry Volunteers'. Janet, an attractive, somewhat nervous woman, viewed this development with dismay. Having recently lost a brother in the Indian Mutiny, she was wary about colonial race relations. A war in Taranaki between government troops and followers of the Māori King had ended the previous March. In Janet's view, it did not bode well that almost immediately upon arrival, her husband had signed up for active service in any future conflicts.

In Napier, William met and took them to the Masonic Hotel,

where they intended to stay a few days. James would soon arrive and take them to Clifton. Meanwhile, they relaxed and took their bearings. After the wait in Wellington, and the uncomfortable sea voyage to New Zealand, it must have been a relief to be on firm ground and in Hawke's Bay. During the long ocean journey, living in cramped conditions they'd had plenty of time to wonder about the remote unknown country where they planned to start a new life. Now they were finally in the vicinity of their future home.

Napier turned out to be a lively, sociable place. Thomas used this time to introduce himself to the local military establishment at Onepoto Gully, at the western end of Scinde Hill. He immediately forged a strong bond with Lieutenant (later Captain) Kenrick Hill, a Northern Irishman who had arrived in New Zealand with the 14th Regiment in 1860. This friendship proved to be life-long and mutually rewarding. The two men both had military careers and a love of the outdoors in common: they enjoyed duck shooting together on the estuary one evening. The next night Hill and his pretty young wife, Elizabeth, hosted a dinner party, introducing Thomas and Janet to the Ashton St Hills, their neighbours on Tuki Tuki Station, Braithwaite, the local bank manager, and Thomas

ABOVE LEFT
JG Gordon as a young man with his wife Elizabeth and sons William and Thomas, 1830s.
GORDON FAMILY COLLECTION

ABOVE RIGHT
Portrait of Captain Thomas Edward Gordon by Major Hopkins, 1876.
GORDON FAMILY COLLECTION

Tanner, a wealthy pastoralist and businessman. Janet felt heartened by Napier's apparent friendliness and hospitality. Thomas was pleased to find considerable local support for his volunteer cavalry troop. Less positively, William had disappeared after booking them into the hotel and had not been seen since. He may have been frequenting local pubs. Feeling ever more negative about his new occupation, he'd started drinking heavily.

Upon arrival, Janet found a comfortable, charming house familiar in design, being similar to ones in India.

James duly arrived and drove them to Clifton. Upon arrival, Janet found a comfortable, charming house that was familiar in design, being similar to ones in India. Nestled against bush-clad hills and facing the ocean, its setting was undeniably picturesque, but must have seemed very lonely and quiet compared to India, despite the fact that there were towns and pastoral estates not far away. She looked forward to setting up a garden, but realised that, being so close to the sea, that might be challenging. Thomas promised her a full-time gardener to help get one established. She soon became pregnant, however, and the garden's attractions weakened. Her sense of isolation grew. When Thomas wasn't out killing pigs with William, he was tending to farming matters, or training his cavalry volunteers in a field near the Meeanee Hotel. Their drills were a bit primitive, with only sticks to practise sword exercises, and eventually the troop disbanded. Janet worried about the increasingly tense relations between the colonial government and the Māori King movement, and the impact any conflict might have on her family. She gave birth to her first child, Edward, in 1863, the year that Governor George Grey's forces invaded the Waikato, ushering in the longest and most important of the New Zealand Wars. She gave birth to her second child, Helen, in 1864, the year that clash ended and the Māori King and his followers withdrew to the King Country. Another son, Frank, arrived in 1865, by which time the wars had entered a new phase of more sporadic, localised campaigns.

Despite worries about the possibility of further wars, Janet's life with Thomas at Clifton was frequently busy and happy. What with the distance and the unpredictable river crossings, entertaining at home was difficult but not impossible or infrequent. The beach was a great attraction during summer, and family and visiting friends enjoyed walks and picnics under the majestic coastal cliffs of the peninsula or up the river gullies. The Hills visited regularly, and Kenrick and Thomas hunted pigs at Clifton or shot ducks and pukeko together on Napier waters. Kenrick increasingly helped Thomas out with key tasks at the station, such as mustering the Cape country for shearing. This involved riding out with the shepherds and dogs, camping in the basin at the head of Porpoise Gully, then bringing the sheep back to Clifton following the shoreline beneath the cliffs. An added complication of this route was the absolute necessity of getting the tides right. If that was not timed perfectly, it meant camping out with the sheep until the way was safe and clear. Thomas, when not engaged on the farm, accompanied his wife, who relished Napier's social whirl; from Race Days, when everyone dressed in their finest apparel, to dinner parties at the Braithwaites and the Hills, to picnics at the Spit, to 'at home' teas with local ladies such as Mrs St Hill and Mrs Tanner.

THE TWELVE APOSTLES AND FERNHILL

In 1865, Julia Tanner's redoubtable husband, Thomas, approached the Gordons about a syndicate he was forming to lease 17,785 acres (7200 hectares) of the Heretaunga Plains. This was the beginning of the 'Twelve Apostles' affair, a land transaction that attracted nationwide notoriety. The name was something of a misnomer, as there were never 12 apostles; rather seven men who between them held 12 shares of the Heretaunga Block. Falling wool prices and a recession in the late 1860s had encouraged run-holders to look for more productive land, and the plains were the only unoccupied land in Hawke's Bay suitable for grazing except in the backcountry ranges. James acquired two shares and immediately handed them over to

Thomas. Other syndicate members included prominent pastoralists such as JD Ormond and Purvis Russell. Having drawn lots at the Hawke's Bay Club for the surveyed blocks, the 'Apostles' began fencing, draining swamps, and building yards on their new leasehold properties. From 1865, Tanner leased the land from its Māori owners: two years later a Crown grant legalised the arrangement. A clause in the lease stating improvements could be deducted from rents meant the Apostles had the land virtually rent-free.

Over the next few years the 10 Māori owners listed on the Crown grant were pressured to sell by various means, notably debt. Two storekeepers in particular, Frederick Sutton and RD Maney, let the Māori owners build up debts that they could only pay by relinquishing land. The rangatira Karaitiana Takamoana reluctantly sold the last share of the block in 1870. In all, 17,785 acres sold for £19,920. This was not particularly cheap, nor was the means of obtaining the sale at all atypical at the time, yet the Apostles attracted criticism in the press and elsewhere. This was partly due to growing opposition towards run-holders and their control of provincial politics, and the view that closer settlement of agriculture would help solve unemployment and end recession. As the historian Mary Boyd observed: 'The lessees of the Heretaunga block faced it full blast.' The purchase also became a handy political football in the early 1870s, when the pastoralist and provincial politician Henry Russell decried it, part of his motivation being to undermine his arch-enemy, JD Ormond. Russell helped found and finance the Hawke's Bay Repudiation Movement, a cause that, drawing on Māori anger over land alienation, called for the repudiation of all Crown land deals on the basis of fraud. In 1873 the Hawke's Bay Native Lands Alienation Commission, after investigating the Twelve Apostles case, vindicated the purchasers, concluding that there was only minimal foul play. But public criticisms and resentment over the Heretaunga purchase continued, and as late as 1880 the Apostles paid a further £5000 for a deed of confirmation to the title.

In 1865, when the entrepreneurial Tanner proposed the syndicate to James and Thomas, this negative publicity and ongoing strife were not foreseeable. Rather, it seemed an opportunity to acquire potentially productive land. The Gordons paid £3320 for the 3462-acre (1400-hectare) Fernhill Block. In 1866 they also purchased the

300-acre (120-hectare) Ranga Ika reserve on Te Matau-a-Māui for £100. They had leased this land since the early 1860s, from Karauria, a local rangatira who, like the owners of the Heretaunga Block and many others in the locality, now needed to sell it to pay off pressing debts.

TIPPING POINT: 1866

In the opening months of 1866, James's plan to rebuild the family fortunes was paying off handsomely. Clifton had started to produce a good income, and there were now 11,813 sheep on the property. He and his sons owned a comfortable homestead; he had three healthy New Zealand-born grandchildren, a housekeeper to look after his needs, and the Hawke's Bay Club in Napier where he could play billiards to his heart's content.

However, this rosy picture darkened as the year progressed. On 21 March, a messenger appeared at the house with news that William had drowned. After an evening of drinking in Napier, he'd fallen off his horse into the Meeanee Stream. His body was found the next morning. James must have experienced this loss keenly, and felt some burden of responsibility. After all, his sheep-farming scheme had uprooted his elder son from everything he knew and loved. William never warmed to Clifton, missing the rituals and camaraderie of army life in India. He'd died in a manner that was all too common in the colony at the time, alone and inebriated, on horseback, crossing a body of water. He was only 36 years old.

After William's death, James's hopes for the future rested with his younger son. Thomas, energetic and capable, in contrast to William, enjoyed station life and actively and happily engaged with farming. Janet, however, still felt insecure in the new environment, unsettled by newspaper reports of conflict and tensions between Māori and Pākehā around the country. In February 1865, a small band of Hauhau had moved into Hawke's Bay, welcomed by Te Hapuku, who hoped to use them in his power struggles with other local rangatira. The Hauhau or Pai Marire movement, which spread rapidly in the early 1860s, followed the teachings of a self-proclaimed prophet called Te Ua Haumene. Te Ua taught that Māori, a lost tribe of Israel held in bondage by Pākehā, needed to drive all non-Māori out of Aotearoa.

ABOVE
Oamanui [Ōmarunui] *after the Fight* (12 October 1866), a watercolour painted by Edward Lyndon in 1866.
ALEXANDER TURNBULL LIBRARY, WELLINGTON, NZ: A-196-008

True believers would be immune to bullets by raising their right hand; those who died had not sufficient faith.

The arrival of Hauhau aroused settler fears, which turned to alarm after Hauhau murdered Reverend Carl Völkner at Ōpōtiki in March. Many local Māori were also dismayed. The chief Karaitiana Takamoana, a devout Christian, wrote to the *Evening Post* on 28 March 1865 expressing 'our unmeasured distress' at 'those murderers'. Other local rangatira such as Tareha and Renata Kawepo agreed with him: by mid-1866 the only Hauhau in the region were Ngāti Hineuru, based at Te Haroto and Tarawera on the track to Taupo. But in early October, a fully armed group led by the prophet Panapa marched from Te Haroto. Some 25 men, under the warrior Te Rangihiroa, remained at Petane (now Bay View). The rest, a large group including women and children, set themselves up in the unfortified pā at Ōmarunui on the Tutaekuri River (some 13 kilometres south-west of Napier).

Hawke's Bay was now on tenterhooks, aware that battle might commence any day. According to reports from local Māori, the armed group intended to invade Napier and kill all of its inhabitants. Thomas later wrote an account describing a frightening event that occurred at Clifton at this time, and his experience of the major battle the following day:

> *One afternoon my father and I noticed a cloud of dust on the road about a mile off and soon a swarm of Hau haus some 20 to 25 galloped up to the house, got off their horses, and came onto the verandah and then invaded the house, one fellow taking up a carving knife and examining it. This was not very nice and alarmed my wife. After a time I said to my father – we must show a bold front and we set to work and pushed them off the verandah and after saying something in Māori – which I afterwards learned was 'wait a bit', they galloped off.*
>
> *The next day I galloped into Napier to see what was going on and called on Colonel Sir George Whitmore commanding the Colonial Forces, who happened to be there. He said 'We are going to take the Militia out tonight and attack the Hau haus who have taken possession of Omarunui.'*

Thomas was ordered to reactivate his volunteer cavalry troop. He quickly assembled 20 men, issuing them real rifles rather than sticks this time. At 10pm on 11 October they set off for the cliffs at Poraiti, where it was believed more canoes might land with reinforcements. They left in pitch dark, but luckily some men knew the country, so they travelled in a straight line to their destination. When dawn broke, there was no sign of any canoes. Thomas sent a messenger to Whitmore asking if his men could return to the main force. He agreed. They cantered quickly back, hearing gunfire as they rode. When they returned, the battle of Ōmarunui was in full pitch. Whitmore's troops numbered 175, and there were some 200 Māori under Tareha Te Moananui and Renata Kawepo fighting with the government forces. The Hauhau, heavily outnumbered, battled for some time, but eventually raised a white flag. Some 13 or 14 escaped, and Thomas and his men immediately mounted their horses, crossed the river and gave chase. They did not get far, however, before a messenger arrived saying that, the battle being conclusively won, McLean did not want any more bloodshed.

Upon returning to Ōmarunui, Thomas found the Clifton gardener, George Stevens, lying on the ground in pain, having been shot in the lower jaw during battle. 'What in the world are you doing here?' Thomas asked, shocked. He was informed that all male employees had been rounded up from Clifton Station for military service soon after he'd left for Napier. His account continues:

> *I made arrangements at his request for my gardener to be taken home instead of to the Hospital and got leave from Colonel Whitmore to hand over the troop to my lieutenant to take back to Napier. I galloped home to relieve my wife and father and to break the news to the gardener's wife. The poor man was many months before he was fit for work and he said to me, 'I came to New Zealand to garden, sir, and not to fight!'*

Although Thomas survived the battle of Ōmarunui unscathed, Janet remained anxious. Scotland seemed a much safer environment for her family than Hawke's Bay. In 1867 Thomas and Janet returned permanently to Scotland. Thomas asked his friend Kenrick Hill to move onto Clifton and manage the station. James remained with the Hills, in self-contained quarters, replete with the cast-iron bath from India. After Janet died giving birth to her sixth child in 1869, Thomas visited Clifton a year later, aiming to persuade James to return to Scotland. He spent over two years at the station, helping to sort out various farming and financial matters.

DRAMAS AND DELIGHTS: THE HILLS AT CLIFTON, 1867–88

Thomas's visit features in Elizabeth Hill's diary. For over a 20-year period this daily journal chronicled her busy life as mistress of Clifton. When she and Kenrick moved there in April 1867, she had a month-old daughter, Kathleen; a son, Dudley, arrived in 1869. The diary records a succession of domestic dramas, as well as the pleasures, perils and work routines of station life. Crossing, or attempting to cross, the Tukituki features regularly:

[April 1871] Drove to town, just two months since I was there, river still very high. The grey mare started plunging in the river, got such a fright.

[20 May] Crossed the river in a boat, and drove to town in a hired trap . . . Ken and Captain Gordon went down to the club in the evening to play billiards.

[2 July] Ken and Captain Gordon tried to cross the river but had to come back, it was so high.

[19 June 1875] Pouring rain. The dray came back, it got stuck in the river here [the Maraetotara] and everything washed out of it.

[20 June] Went for a walk and saw floods of water all over the paddocks. They got a lot of things out of the river. Spread out the raisins and currants to dry.

Although she had domestic servants, several of whom proved 'impudent' or problematic, Elizabeth herself did all manner of chores. She turned her hand to mangling laundry, churning butter, picking and bottling fruit, making jam, sewing clothes for the children and herself, feeding hens and gathering eggs, and looking after various pets, including a succession of dogs – several had to be shot for attacking sheep – to canaries and one 'wicked little parrot'. The diary also gives an insight into the annual cycle of farming duties the men engaged in, from docking to shearing:

[October 1872] Docking all day. Captain Russell, Mr. Hood's son and Maclean all came to dinner. Ken is going to join the Gordons at Karamu [Fernhill]. On the 10th began shearing at eleven, did 500. The shearers get their meals up here, gave them a dozen eggs. On the 15th still shearing, shore 900. Kathleen not at all well. Sewed a serge frock for Dudley. On the 28th finished shearing. Captain Gordon went to the Karamu in the dray with things.

In the course of his extended visit to Clifton in 1872, Thomas took part in all of the activities of the station, hunted pigs with Kenrick,

ABOVE
The Hill family.
HILL FAMILY COLLECTION

and bought a horse and trap, which made the journey to the river more comfortable. He eventually succeeded in persuading James, 79, to return with him to North Devon, where the family now lived, and the two left together in April 1873. In September 1872 Elizabeth noted in the diary: 'Got the bath taken out of old Mr. Gordon's room at last.'

Although now living far away, James and Thomas could take heart in Clifton's prosperity. Productivity increased steadily. By 1871, the station boasted 16,778 sheep. Eventually, Lincoln rams, purchased in 1881, produced larger sheep better suited to the rugged country. From 1878, Shorthorn cattle were introduced both at Clifton and Fernhill. Increased stock and productivity called for more horses, which were then integral to farming. Their oats grew in a paddock at Te Awanga, and the horses lived in a new two-storey stable on the roadside, as well as another stable with a loft across the road. Newly planted trees around the homestead, mostly pine and gum, provided shelter and shade. Behind the house a new residence for

shepherds became known as 'Bachelors' Cottage'. Further up the drive the gardener and his family lived in another recently completed purpose-built house. These buildings, constructed from New Zealand hardwood, with mataī flooring and rimu walls and ceilings, proved attractive and enduring. At the Ocean Beach end of the property, another new cottage housed a permanent shepherd.

In 1877, the Hills built a summer cottage at Mataurau, on the Ocean Beach side of the property, where they swam and enjoyed the sweep of golden sand and the craggy cliffs behind. They also regularly picnicked at various scenic spots around the station, with numerous excursions around to Black Reef, and up the gullies leading over to the river.

In May 1879 Thomas returned to Clifton for another visit. He was now 51, and as Elizabeth noted in her diary: 'Captain Gordon has gone quite grey.' He had buried his father, James, in September 1878, and perhaps welcomed the change of scene. After a busy, active time, hunting with Kenrick, going to the Tanners to shoot, and seeing old friends, he departed in May 1880. The Hills themselves

ABOVE
Bachelors' Cottage, 1870.
GORDON FAMILY COLLECTION

ABOVE
A young Frank Gordon.
GORDON FAMILY COLLECTION

then travelled abroad from 1881 to 1884, ending their journey with a visit to Thomas in Devon. They returned to Clifton on 21 January 1884. Elizabeth described the homecoming in her diary:

> We started at 11.30 in the train (along the foreshore to Clive). Jack had a trap at Clive, Tom and Frank rode, we took Beau with us. The trees have grown a great deal, but the garden is a wilderness, no fruit or anything . . . We are glad to be back again.

The Frank accompanying them was Frank Gordon, Thomas's son. Handsome, energetic and 19 years old, he aimed, under Kenrick's guidance, to learn farming. Immediately thrust into station working life, he proved a quick learner, riding out to muster, helping to restore the garden and, in time-honoured fashion, shooting wild pigs. Elizabeth's diary notes the addition of a 'beautiful' fountain – now long-gone – in front of the house, as well as the acquisition of a 'handsome' piano, and the creation of a tennis court and several garden paths. Although this was a time of widespread economic depression, Clifton's balance books appear to have been sufficiently in the black to accommodate such expenditure. In 1885, Frank welcomed his friend and first cousin Pat Robertson to the station, who joined him as a cadet. The two young men worked hard, sometimes at Fernhill as well as at Clifton, but also found time to visit friends, play tennis, attend dances and dinner parties, and, with the Hills, set up a new camp between the Cape and the Black Reef. In September 1886, Thomas arrived with his youngest son, Charlie, who also started working on the station as a cadet. There were now 25,000 sheep on the property.

Around this time, Thomas must have informed the Hills that Frank would soon take over running the station on behalf of the Gordon family. By late October the Hills were living in the Grange as an interim measure before moving to Fernhill. In February 1887, they farewelled Thomas with a dinner party, and in May moved into a newly built family home, Fernhill House. Some years later, in 1892, Thomas sold his share of Fernhill to Kenrick on very fair terms, aware that he owed his friend a debt of gratitude for helping Clifton prosper over a formative 20-year period. Thomas's departure in 1888 marked the beginning of a new era. Clifton was now in Frank Gordon's capable hands.

ABOVE
The stable and single man's quarters seen from the driveway to the house.
GORDON FAMILY COLLECTION

Red Letter Day: The Black Bridge Opens

On 9 May 1888, the long-awaited bridge over the Tukituki River finally opened. Officially called the Grange Bridge, but soon dubbed the Black Bridge by locals, it was built by the county council, which borrowed £9000 from the government for the purpose. The owners of the three stations on the Kidnappers side of the river – Clifton, Clive Grange and Tuki Tuki – happily paid for the interest on the loan, grateful that, at last, all the uncertainties and potential danger of attempting to cross the river were at an end. The person who opened this facility, Miss Ellen Tanner, later became Mrs Frank Gordon.

ABOVE
The old Black Bridge and its successor, built in 1956, in the foreground.
GORDON FAMILY COLLECTION

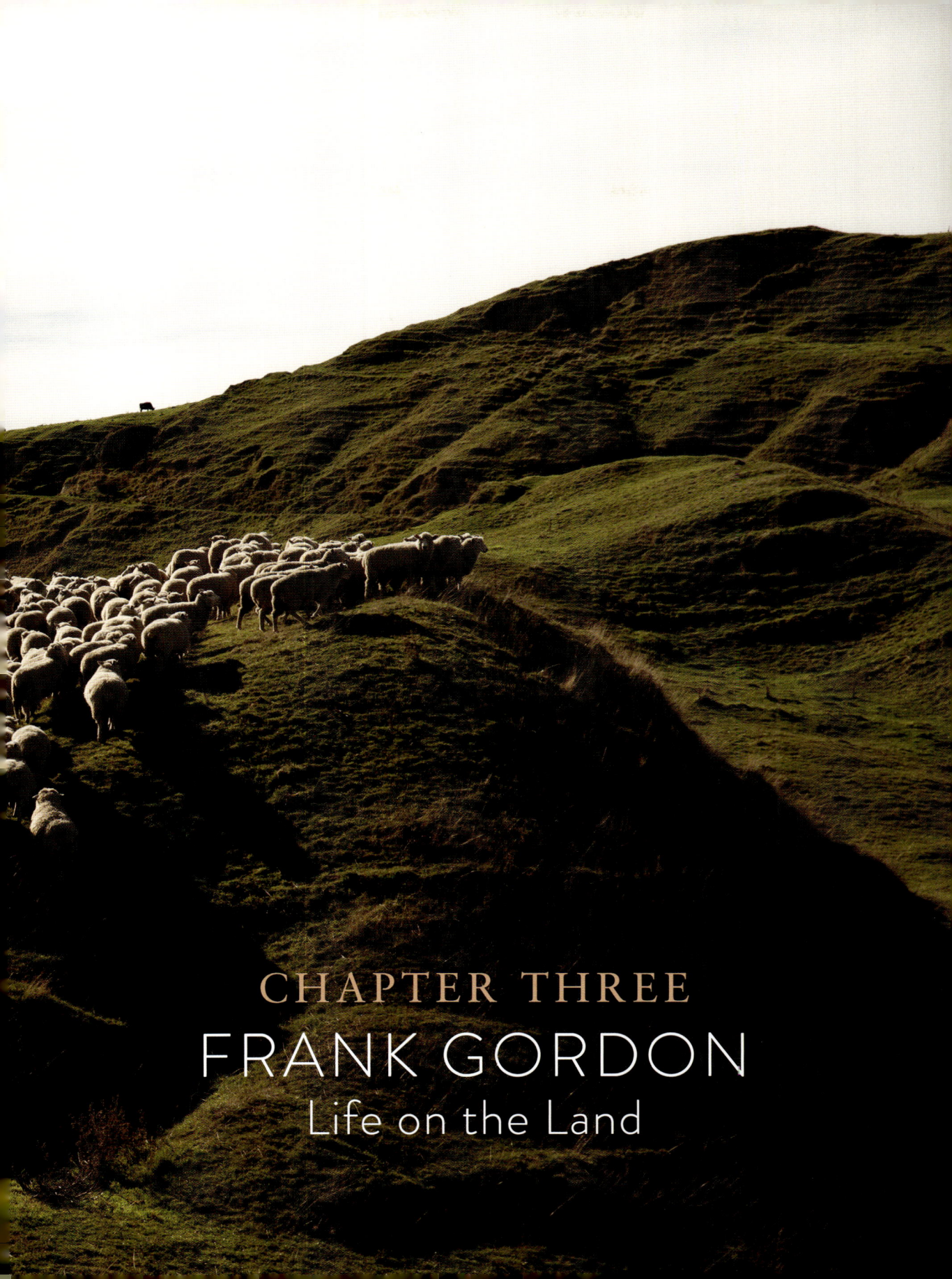

CHAPTER THREE

FRANK GORDON

Life on the Land

Frank Gordon took over managing Clifton in 1888, aged 23. To successfully run such a vast, rugged and challenging station he needed to be physically robust and mentally resilient, to think ahead, solve problems great and small, embrace changing technology and be a fair employer. Luckily he had all of these qualities in abundance. Developing and improving the vast station became his life's work, and he proved admirably suited to the challenge. Writing to his father in 1889, he emphasised how grateful he and his brother Charlie were to be working the land, and keen to prove themselves worthy:

> *I only trust that I can wipe off your debt in a few years and you will be able to have more comfort, as you have treated us both well and we must try and see if we cannot let you reap the benefit of it by making this place pay better than it has been doing . . .*

Frank began farming Clifton at a fortunate time. From the mid-1890s until the early 1920s, New Zealand agriculture entered a golden age. Refrigeration transformed the economy. The most important new industry in Hawke's Bay was the freezing works established by William Nelson at Tomoana in 1884. In the first season, some 41,000 sheep were exported. Wool, no longer the sole export staple, now shared the stage with meat and dairy produce. Before the advent of freezing, surplus or cull sheep had a limited market after shearing. Most were sold to the hide and tallow works near Clive, to be boiled down for tallow. Now, although exporting wool remained Clifton's mainstay, sales of sheep and cattle to Nelson Brothers in Hastings

ABOVE
A wood engraving (artist unknown) of Tomoana freezing works near Hastings, owned by Nelson Brothers, c. 1893.
ALEXANDER TURNBULL LIBRARY, WELLINGTON, NZ: PUBL-0140-1

offered a welcome additional revenue stream. Despite the buoyant rural sector, however, running Clifton inevitably involved challenges and crises. Profits increased, but the daily running of Clifton involved a series of hurdles, great and small, and the need for various costly 'improvements'.

'IMPROVEMENTS THAT PAY WELL FOR DOING'

Frank wrote home regularly to his father about plans to improve the station. As Clifton's owner, Thomas had to approve any expenditure, so Frank's letters often argued the benefits of further investment. He knew that this was necessary if profits were to improve. In January 1889, for example, he responded defensively to a recent letter from AL Elder and Co (the station's bankers and agents in London), which queried the amount spent on 'Improvements':

ABOVE
Portrait of
Frank Gordon
from Clifton,
c. 1910.
GORDON FAMILY
COLLECTION

I quite agree with what Elder says about the Improvements, and if I had thought two years ago that we were going to go too heavy into Improvements, I should never have thought of ploughing, but having gone half way now, I must finish. The fences which have gone up this last two years have enabled us as you see to carry about 3000 more sheep in the winter and with this increase you must remember that it is cross-bred sheep, which take more keeping and looking after, but at the same time give a bigger return. I sold 1200 merino wethers this year at 5 shillings which realize £300, the same number last year would have fetched us in £240.

Now Nelson [Brothers] would not have given 5 shillings for those sheep unless they had been really fat and we could not have topped them off only for the rape, so I think that was well spent time and money. We have weaned the weakest of the lambs on to it now . . . I will try my best to make the place pay and at the same time make a few improvements as it would look as if the place had come to a standstill.

Over the next few years Frank certainly did not allow the place to come to a standstill, but continued busily improving, starting a waterworks programme on the hill behind the house, burning off fern in the Rabbit Gully area, then planting grass in late winter to guarantee moisture. Writing to Thomas in April 1889, he both complains about a current drought and tells of steps he's taking to prevent the flood damage experienced last year:

We are having a fearful season the longest without rain we have had yet . . . We start dipping on Monday and thank goodness as it is a regular hanging on season waiting for rain . . . As for ploughing it is out of the question, I have taken this opportunity to have the place tidied up and then we may be able to keep it tidy . . . I am going to put the cow pad in oats again this year as I think I am too late for grass now. I am having it ploughed about 3 inches deep now . . . I have had a drain dug right through the low part and hope to save it being flooded like it was last year . . .

In 1892 he and Ebbett, his head shepherd, subdivided the outstation side of the station into five blocks with 5 miles (8 kilometres) of fencing and erected 3 miles (4.8 kilometres) of fencing on the Cape side. Frank planted 20 more apple trees around the Bachelors' Cottage and some orange and lemon trees. The lemons proved a good investment:

I don't know what we would have done without them through all this sickness we have had on the place lately. Fourteen cases of influenza, everything seemed upside down and nothing seemed to be going on. First a drayman, then the gardener, Mrs. McCormick and four kids, Ebbett, his wife and three kids, and Irvine. They are all on the mend now but a bit weak.

At the beginning of 1893, there were 20,226 sheep on Clifton, not including 400 missing lambs. To counter footrot, the ewes were walked through arsenic troughs at the woolshed yards and at the outstation. Later in the year Thomas, who was moving into and upgrading a house in Devon and therefore more than usually cost-conscious, wrote querying the need for more fencing. Again, Frank argued his case persuasively:

I can assure you the extra convenience in mustering is a great thing. To show you what I mean we have been dagging all last week, we started on the ewes which are on the new country, we had all the ewes which were out there in and out again in a week (7500). Considering I only had 4 men on the board for 3 days, and 9 men on the other 4 we did not do so badly. It kept 3 shepherds doing nothing else but bringing in and taking out and two of us at the foot rot trough. Now before it was fenced it was a case of getting the whole mob in at once and eating us out of house and home before a week was out and if bad weather caught us it was a case of starve them for an extra day or two. That is my reason for putting up yards at the back for one thing and also the saving to the sheep of driving them all the way here to take them back . . . Now these are the sorts of improvements that pay well for doing.

Frank went on to assure his father that wool had sold well that year and they would net £700 more than the previous year. He also reassured him that the overdraft would only be temporary, as they were going to be carrying some 2000 more sheep the next winter. The often defensive or complaining tone of Frank's letters sometimes obscures the fact that Clifton under his vigilant care was doing very well. Wool output rose significantly. In November 1888 Frank sent 308 bales of greasy wool to England. In 1889 he sent 337, in 1891, 342; in 1892, 392 bales. Clifton was a profitable, productive station, and Frank's steady 'Improvements' helped it to flourish.

MARRIAGE AND CHILDREN

In addition to his busy work schedule, Frank somehow found time to court his friend Errington Tanner's lively and attractive sister Ellen (always known as Nelly to friends and family). On 16 April 1891 they married at St Luke's Anglican Church in Havelock North. The officiating minister, Rev Canon St Hill, was both the bride's uncle and the scion of another pioneering Hawke's Bay pastoralist family. A reporter describing the event in the *Daily Telegraph* noted reverentially: 'From the position of the parties, and wide respect for them, especially Mr Tanner, it is superfluous to state that the church was crowded. The vehicles were so numerous that it was almost useless to try to count them.'

The wedding reception took place at Riverslea, the bride's gracious 22-room family home. Her father, Thomas, hosted the occasion with characteristic generosity and panache. Self-confident and often recklessly entrepreneurial, Tanner (known as 'Tizzy' to his detractors), his wife, Julia, and their nine children lived in considerable opulence on the Riverslea Estate. Family life was not without its ups and downs, however, as Thomas's numerous business schemes frequently ended disastrously. His financial affairs eventually

became so fraught that he had to sell large sections of the Riverslea Estate. In 1896, the Riverslea homestead burnt down completely, and Tanner and Julia moved into a townhouse on Napier Hill. In contrast to his father-in-law's varied speculations and business ventures, Frank focused all of his energy on just one end: Clifton. He knew that ultimately how well he managed it directly affected his family in England, who relied on its income. Meanwhile, his immediate family in New Zealand began growing. He and Nelly's first child, a daughter, Eileen, arrived in September 1892, followed by Thomas Lindsay – always known as Lindsay – in August 1894.

PROBLEMS AND SOLUTIONS: TAURAPA

Lindsay's birth was a bright point in a challenging year. Wool prices fell and Frank lost a disastrous 3000 hoggets in winter. Writing to

ABOVE
Riverslea homestead, the luxurious mansion Tanner built for his family on his Riverslea Estate, 1890.
GORDON FAMILY COLLECTION

Elders in November 1894 about this significant loss, he observed:

> *I am sorry to say though we started with a good mob of hoggets in the Autumn we were very short at shearing time. I knew we were losing a good many by the skins that came in, but was surprised to find we had lost nearly 3000 and consequently we are short of bales.*
>
> *We never did more for the young sheep than we did this year and it seemed all for no good.*
>
> *I believe nearly everyone in the province are short of both wool and sheep.*

Thomas wrote, again concerned about the station's debt levels. Meanwhile Frank's younger brother Charlie, hankering after his own land, grew increasingly disaffected. To prevent future hogget losses, Frank began a rigorous dosing programme. This practice had numerous detractors among the farming community at the time, but Frank strongly believed in it. He financed the process out of his own

ABOVE
The old stables at Clifton.

ABOVE
The Gordons, 1896. Seated at front, left to right: Thomas, Lindsay, Nelly, Frank and Eileen; seated behind: Bessie and Charlie.
GORDON FAMILY COLLECTION

OPPOSITE TOP
Bringing sheep around the beach to the woolshed.
GORDON FAMILY COLLECTION

OPPOSITE BOTTOM
Twenty blade shearers, plus shed-hands, shepherds and general hands, 1893.
GORDON FAMILY COLLECTION

pocket and his faith proved justified: stock losses decreased.

The problem of what to do about Charlie was settled in July 1895, when Thomas agreed to Frank's proposal to give him 1640 acres (663 hectares) at the back of Clifton, on the Maraetotara River side. They named it Taurapa, which means 'the carved stern of the war canoe': the Māori name for the highest hill on the land. The block, some of the best country on the station, was a present to mark Charlie's impending wedding to Elizabeth (Bessie) Campbell of Christchurch. It would be his own land, without a mortgage but with a small lease to pay to his father. In 1896, Thomas, aged 68, spent three months visiting New Zealand to attend the wedding and oversee the final arrangements about Taurapa.

This was the first, but not the last, subdivision of Clifton Station. Politically, the times were not sympathetic to vast rural properties. From the 1880s onwards, the Liberals under John Ballance vowed to bust up the big estates and put small-holders on the land. A series of measures to persuade big landowners to reduce their holdings came into effect, from a tax on the unimproved value of land valued at over £500, to a graduated tax starting at 1/8d in the pound rising to 2d on estates worth £5000 or more. Absentee owners such as Thomas paid

OPPOSITE TOP
This Māori gang from Waimarama did the shearing at Taurapa for years.
MICHAEL GORDON COLLECTION

OPPOSITE BOTTOM
Taurapa wool going out, 1920.
MICHAEL GORDON COLLECTION

ABOVE
Romney two-tooths coming into the yards, 1890s.
GORDON FAMILY COLLECTION

a further 20 per cent. Later, when Richard Seddon became premier, he too advocated closer land settlement. But for the time being, with the exception of Charlie's block, Clifton Station remained in one piece.

Charlie chose a site for his homestead looking north down the river valley and up at the great Taurapa hill. The kauri for his single-storey, 12-room house was brought from Auckland by boat. It was then floated ashore on the tide, pulled high up on the beach, covered with sand and left to season for six weeks before being carted to the site by bullock wagons. Charlie and Bessie eventually raised three children – Mick, Patrick and Ian – in their attractive family home. Charlie also built another house, a rather grand one, for his pigeons. Mick Gordon later remembered that, in uncertain weather, his father usually took some birds with him on the arduous trip into town (this involved wending his way down the hill, then fording the Tukituki River): 'He released one with a message tied to its leg, when he left town, and the second when he reached the Tukituki, to let us know whether it was safe to cross the ford.'

When Charlie moved into Taurapa he benefited from the fact that

ABOVE
Taurapa Homestead, 1896. By the 1890s, there was a bridle track from Havelock to Waimarama and the only coach route was past Taurapa, down to Ocean Beach and then along the beach at low tide.
MICHAEL GORDON COLLECTION

OPPOSITE
Last pig's head (1900) in the hallway at Clifton, with a moose shot by Angus's maternal grandfather, Eddie Herrick, in Fiordland.

Frank had already ploughed and planted some fodder crops on the land. In the course of their farming lives, the two Gordon brothers generally helped each other out as much as possible.

GOOD SPIRITS AND A STATELY NEW HOME

By the late 1890s Frank had pared Clifton's permanent station staff down to four shepherds, a cowman, a gardener, a drayman and himself. He brought in extra labour at shearing and dipping times, and employed gangs of local Māori to help eliminate wild pigs. This worked well – by 1900 the 'Captain Cookers' had disappeared.

In 1897, Frank wrote to his father, now back in Devon, increasingly confident. He'd had a bumper year, earning good prices for his wool, achieving better pasture through good burn-offs and considerably decreasing the station debt:

You will no doubt think I am in perhaps too good spirits, so I am, but I have just cause to be as everything is in good order and I will give you figures for 1897 which I hope will cheer you . . .

After all expenses including Frank's salary, the balance earned at the end of 1897 was £4277, some £206 more than the previous year. If his plans for the future proceeded with some luck, he assured his father, 'New Year's day 1898 will see you £2000 less in debt.' He added, with justifiable pride: 'I learn more every day and hope we may all derive benefit from it.'

In 1898, on Thomas's invitation, Frank and Nelly and the children spent a year in England, meeting the rest of the Gordon family. Charlie looked after Clifton, and a housekeeper took charge of the homestead. Upon learning that Frank and Nelly planned to return, the housekeeper aired and cleaned the house. Unfortunately, as she did so, a lamp fell over, a curtain caught fire and the flames quickly took hold. More fortunately it was late October and shearing time, so some 40 men rushed in from the woolshed and just managed to remove all the furniture, including the original pieces from India, in time.

Frank and Nelly arrived back to the charred remnants of their home. The station had enjoyed some profitable years and insurance money helped recover costs. They began planning the dream home Nelly had always longed for, to be built on the same site.

Having bought matai and rimu, they left it to dry for a year. Local builders Bull Brothers won their first big contract to build the handsome 25-room Edwardian mansion, designed by the respected architect WP Finch. Once the foundations were laid, Frank and Nelly placed some coins in a pipe, then buried it under the first pile as a good-luck token.

In January 1901, they moved into their handsome, stately new home, the realisation of all Nelly's dreams. Decorative fretwork adorned the top of the three-sided verandah. There were high 4.6-metre studs on both storeys, and a kitchen strategically placed to catch the morning sun, with a conservatory on the east side and a stunning view out to sea. Each major room had a fireplace, and each of the five large upstairs bedrooms had a walk-in wardrobe. There was a dining room, a billiards room which doubled as a school-room for Lindsay and Eileen, a morning room for entertaining, and a large office for Frank, replete

OPPOSITE
Clifton homestead.

ABOVE
The Clifton driveway before the public road was put through in 1910.
GORDON FAMILY COLLECTION

with a fire-proof walk-in safe. The kitchen boasted a 1.2-metre 'Orion' cooking stove. The washrooms had white earthenware wash basins with brass plugs and chains, and there were two enamelled 1.8-metre-long iron baths. Both the billiards room and the morning room had attractive alcove windows, with beautiful arches. The staircase and hallway, left in varnished rimu, have never been painted to this day. In 2016, over a hundred years later, the house that Frank and Nelly built remains an attractive family home, elegant, spacious and sound.

RECREATION AND RESPONSIBILITY

By the late 1880s and 1890s, although the heyday of Hawke's Bay sheep farmers had passed, the Gordons continued to prosper and play a significant public role. Frank, for example, served on the Hawke's Bay County Council for 17 years as the member for the Riding of Clive, acting as chairman from 1912 to 1914.

As Clifton's proprietor, he held a prominent position in the local community, employing both domestic and station staff. The number of employees at the station varied, but there were always several permanent shepherds – usually four or five – a 'headman' who could manage the men and make decisions in Frank's absence, a gardener, a drayman, and a station cook. Correspondence in 1910 about hiring a station cook stated that the position involved cooking for seven or eight permanent hands. During shearing, however, there would be 28–30 hungry men, and around 12 during lamb shearing. For both shearings, a mate would assist the cook. The latter's pay during these busy periods was augmented by a pound a week in addition to the usual 30/- weekly. Up to 90 per cent of shearing gangs in Hawke's Bay were Māori; it later became common for gangs to organise their own catering. The Gordons also employed a cook-cum-housekeeper, a housemaid and, for a time, a governess at the homestead.

Frank's letters reveal that he acted fairly towards employees who worked well, but had little patience for those who failed to pull their weight or who caused trouble. His respect for his head shepherd, first Ebbett and later John Sommerville, shines through in his correspondence, as well as his generosity and gratitude towards them. When Ebbett left Clifton and set up on his own land in 1897, Frank wrote to Thomas:

> *Ebbett has gone and knowing you would like to give him a present after so many years service I gave him 100 old ewes from you. I also bought 20 station ewes and 4 Romney Rams and made him a present of them.*

Although county council and station responsibilities occupied much of Frank's energy, he and Nelly also enjoyed an active social life. They joined in the annual round of Hawke's Bay dances, balls, hunting, race weeks in Napier and Hastings, visits with friends, sporting activities, the Hawke's Bay A and P Show every October, and a great many picnics at Clifton and elsewhere.

Frequently, as in James's time, the rivers posed special logistical challenges when attempting to get into town for social events, or to friends' homes for visits. Writing to Thomas in 1893, for example, Frank described attending a ball with Nelly in late June.

The unpredictable waters of the Maraetotara perhaps even added to the fun:

> *[21 June] . . . Nelly and I drove to Hastings to Steeplechase ball.*
>
> *[22 June] Paid off daggers. Shepherds round sheep. We tried to get home but could not, Pat [Robertson] met us with pack horse at bridge with change of things. He nearly had to swim our creek. We went in to town to the Caledonian Ball, which was very good, about 700 or 800 people I should think. I wonder what the Eastbourne folk would think if they saw Nelly dancing reels etc with kilted gents. Fine day.*

In that particular instance, the demands of the station fitted well between social engagements, but that was not always the case. In April 1894, for example, everyone working on the station missed the Hawke's Bay Easter festivities (which stretched over 10 days and included six days of racing, Caledonian sports, three dances

ABOVE
Picnic at Clifton in the 1890s.
GORDON FAMILY COLLECTION

ABOVE
Frank and horse.
GORDON FAMILY COLLECTION

and two thoroughbred sales) because they were still dipping and burning. At other times, leisure dovetailed with station work. In the early 1890s, Frank acquired two greyhounds, and he, Charlie Tanner, Pat Robertson and Ned Poulton spent some happy times on the land coursing after the increasingly problematic hares and rabbits.

By the early 1900s Frank's letters to his father, although still predominantly concerned with practical matters, often closed on a personal note, with references to the children's progress in riding and sports. In 1902 he writes:

> *Our team of horses was very successful at the [Agricultural] Show . . . Lindsay's pony ridden by Eileen got first and he got a nice little cup with the money; Eileen's pony ridden by one of Smith girls [cousins] only got highly commended.*

In 1904, when Eileen was 12, father, daughter and a female cousin embarked on a five-day trip to Tarawera along the Taupo Road. As he proudly informed Thomas: 'The little girls were not a bit tired although from Hastings the first day was over 40 miles, what would they think of a child in England riding 40 miles in a day?'

Horses were not only essential to running the station but also a source of recreation and pleasure. Frank took pride in his horses, and both Nelly and Eileen were successful competitive horsewomen.

A talent for golf also ran in the family. Thomas remained an accomplished golfer into his eighties, and Frank played regularly to a very high standard, winning the Hawke's Bay Open Golf Championship in 1894. Frank eventually built a six-hole golf course on the front lawn at Clifton, where he and Lindsay enjoyed practising together.

In addition to vegetables from the gardens and fruit from the orchards, hunting and fishing produced a considerable amount of what the family ate at Clifton.

Sheep farming often thwarted Frank's golfing ambitions, however. In 1904 he complained to Thomas that he wouldn't be able to play in April, when the season commenced, as he would be crutching. On the positive side, he noted that his gardener, Rodolph Sturm, had produced a prize-winning collection of vegetables and potatoes at the annual Hawke's Bay A and P Show. Sturm was a descendent of Austrian-born Frederick Sturm, a pioneering horticulturalist and one of the first Europeans to live in Hawke's Bay.

In addition to vegetables from the gardens and fruit from the orchards, hunting and fishing produced a considerable amount of what the family ate at Clifton. In May 1904, Frank wrote to Thomas:

Our big dam is getting a good shooting ground for ducks. I have got 18 today and there must have been 150 on it, but unluckily the wind was blowing the wrong way and they smelt me. I am going to feed them a bit from this [time] on and hope to keep the house supplied through the season.

In the same letter, he tells how Lindsay and his cousins made a healthy profit from catching mice and rats:

> *Harry Smith and Rose [née Tanner] start for home this week and we have two of the boys here for the holidays. They all have great sport ratting, eeling, mousing and spearing flounders. I have had to lower the price of mice from 3d to 1d as the first day they got 23 at 3d and 3 rats at 1/- and on the second day secured 34 mice; yesterday they got 2 nice flounders and a lot of eels . . .*

In summer, Clifton's beaches attracted friends and family. Visitors enjoyed picnics throughout the season, but Nelly's New Year's party was a much-anticipated annual event. Visitors slept in tents set up on the lawn, went on lavish picnics in drays, enjoyed an enormous bonfire on the beach on New Year's Eve, and attended the races on New Year's Day. Over 30 people usually attended, including family and close friends such as the Russells and the Hills. Station life had its challenges, but it also offered rich rewards.

MODERN TIMES: MECHANISED SHEARING, TELEPHONES, CARS

In 1903, Frank, always keen to try innovative technology, wrote to convince Thomas about the need to install shearing machines. These, he argued, would soon become the norm: investing in 12 machines before the next main shearing would ultimately save money. Shearing would take less time; they would only need 12 as opposed to 20 shearers, and have fewer mouths to feed during the work period. Thomas agreed. After first using the new machines for crutching in May 1904, Frank reported triumphantly:

> *You will be glad to hear that we had not one hitch from start to finish and the engine worked splendidly. It takes about 4 gal of oil to run out eight hours and will take about 6 when all the machines are going at a cost of from 1/8 to 1/3 per gal. There is no doubt that they make a fine clean job of the crutching and I*

should think that the sheep ought to last clean at least 2 months longer than with the hand shears.

The machines also worked well during the first main shearing in October. Unfortunately it rained so heavily that year, that what should have taken 10 days took three-and-a-half weeks.

Around this time, Frank installed a telephone line to Clive from the station. J MacFarlane, his new neighbour at Clive Grange, shared the line, thus halving the costs. The whole venture, which covered just over 11 kilometres of line, cost only £31, partly because Frank himself undertook much of the hard labour. This sum, he wrote to Thomas, was money well spent:

Our telephone has been going two weeks now and is a great boon, saving any amount of letter writing and getting a prompt answer which is so satisfactory. If a telegram comes they repeat it to us which is very nice. I expect Charles will be running a wire down to the outstation, it would not cost him much as he could follow the fence most of the way.

Charlie did in fact install a telephone line himself, from Taurapa, across the river and over the Tauroa Road to Havelock North. Undeterred by the river being in flood at the time, he swam a draught horse across the river, paying out the wire as he went.

In 1903 the completion of the Red Bridge over the Tukituki River made car travel feasible. Charlie immediately purchased a Darracq, but the hair-pin bends and steep incline made the trip into town hair-raising, especially in winter. Frank purchased his first car in 1907, a four-seater Wolesley. It was quite high off the ground, which suited his needs, because until 1908, when a bridge was erected over the Maraetotara, he had to ford that river. He never fully mastered driving, and frequently called on Lindsay to do the honours when crossing the river.

In May 1907, Frank wrote to his Aunt Nelly (Janet's widowed sister) in Devon:

Station life is not as simple as it used to be with this machinery, motor cars and acetylene gas, all of which one has to understand

ABOVE
Edward Gordon in 1906, upon his arrival in New Zealand.
GORDON FAMILY COLLECTION

oneself, living in the country. We were stuck up the other night in the dark with the motor taking three hours over twelve miles but we got home and fixed her up the next morning.

In addition to new-fangled shearing machines, telephones and cars, Clifton was changing in other ways as well.

GORDON BROTHERS AND HAUPOURI

On 15 December 1906, Edward Robertson Gordon arrived at Clifton, marking a new stage in Clifton's development. For the past 30 years the station had traded under the name Captain TE Gordon. Henceforward it would be called Gordon Brothers. In 1904, aged 76, Thomas had decided to transfer Clifton to two sons. In doing so he would be liable for gift duty, but the time seemed right, and he was reluctant to pay any further graduated and absentee taxes. Frank and Edward would take mortgages from their father on the land only. In February 1906 Frank travelled to England to discuss these new arrangements with his father directly. He returned to New Zealand in September that year.

Frank and Edward had not met since 1883. It must have been with some relief therefore that Frank wrote to Thomas in January 1907: 'Edward seems to have quite settled down and is easily amused.' At 43, his elder brother, a retired Major and Boer War veteran, was, like Frank, a skilled golfer, and an avid fisherman and hunter – several of his vanquished prey, stuffed and mounted, adorn the hall of Clifton, including a buffalo, a warthog, an alligator and even a pelican.

More punctilious and more fractious than Frank, he was also kind and thoughtful to those he liked and respected. Clouds of Egyptian tobacco smoke frequently wafted out from under the closed door of

'Uncle Edward's room' at the top of the stairs.

In January 1907 surveyors started working on the boundaries of what would now be two properties. By March they had marked out a new boundary, running from the waterfalls on the Maraetotara River to the end of the Whakapau Bluff at the Ranga Ika. Edward's land, which would eventually become Haupouri – which means Dark Water – comprised 4860 acres (1960 hectares); Frank's northern portion, Clifton, was 7000 acres (2830 hectares). Despite the size differential, the winter stock carrying capacity of both properties was the same. Haupouri included some of the best property on the station, while Frank's included the aptly named Rough Block: about 240 hectares of steep ravines and impenetrable kānuka.

ABOVE
John Sommerville started work at Clifton in 1893 as a shepherd on the outstation at Ocean Beach. He remained a trusted employee for 31 years, eventually becoming head shepherd. He capably managed the station whenever Frank was away.
GORDON FAMILY COLLECTION

In winter 1907, Gordon Brothers had 19,000 sheep giving 85 per cent lambing, 1450 cattle and 100 horses. They were doing a lot more trading in older cattle, killing some 300 a year. The annual wool clip averaged 400 bales.

Early in 1908, Nelly travelled to England with the children, whose final years of schooling would be in 'the old country'. It was not uncommon at this time for New Zealanders who had never set foot in Britain to refer to it as 'home', but the Gordons' ties to the mother country remained especially strong. Both Frank and Edward grew up in England; their father, aunts and sisters lived in Devon; wool produced at Clifton ended up in London. Frank frequently purchased materials for the farm in England.

Despite being engaged in the usual hive of activity on the station, Frank missed his family terribly, so in October he left New Zealand to join them. His long-serving, capable head shepherd John Sommerville would manage Clifton day to day; Edward would do the books and take charge when needed.

EDWARD AT THE HELM

From late 1908 until Frank and Nelly's return in 1910, Edward wrote home regularly, providing detailed accounts of Gordon Brothers' expenses and earnings as well as any noteworthy events, crises or dramas. His letters remained calmly matter-of-fact, even occasionally humorous, yet he faced more crises than might reasonably have been anticipated.

One early trouble involved a station employee who accidentally drowned one of Nelly's beloved pet dogs, then failed to admit what he'd done. Much time was wasted, as everyone searched high and low for the long-dead animal. Soon after this, Edward informed Frank:

> *One of these young fellows, putting up the pipes etc., borrowed 'Nora' to go to the [A and P] Show, and was giving her a drink with another horse in the Grand Hotel yard just before starting back when in whizzed a motor. Away went both. They found the other, but ours nowhere although they hunted for her till 1am. Next morning he borrowed a horse and started off to explore and found the mare at that beastly crossing where Crosse came to grief. She had been bowled over by a train and must have been killed on the spot.*

Shearing that year was a nightmare, with ceaseless rain and machine malfunctions. Once finished, John Sommerville and the roustabouts commenced, as per an agreement, to shear sheep from neighbouring properties for a fee. These animals proved so dirty, however, that the shearers demanded more money. Around this time, Sommerville's son Chum, an excellent worker like his father, left (temporarily) to see the world. Poor John felt increasingly stressed and ill from having to make all of the practical decisions in Frank's absence. Writing to his brother, Edward observed: 'Certainly the old man [Sommerville] has been horribly handicapped this summer, both as regards weather and his own health. There is no doubt he wants a thorough change and rest, but you might as well talk to a stone wall as suggest such a thing.' On a positive note, he noted that the wool they'd shipped to London that year had sold very well.

Problems and irritations continued to bubble away. Without

Te Awanga Village

Edward Gordon often got angry about people camping on the boundary of Clifton and the Te Awanga lagoon. Between 1908 and 1909 he and Frank wrote to several families who had been camping on the Clifton side of the river mouth asking them to desist, to no avail. At that time the Burden family had set up a camp and built huts at the river mouth on the Te Awanga side on disputed land. They managed to retain their foothold, and in the 1940s turned it into a commercial camp, which is still operating today.

In 1911 Frank had sold 10 acres (4 hectares) of land on the north side for sections along the road. The village of Te Awanga quickly grew up on the block. In 1914 Frank sold a further 10 acres (4 hectares) bounding the river and the first block, completing the triangle of land that constituted the first settlement of Te Awanga village. In those days, the village was the area between Wellwood Terrace and Clifton Road, including Leyland, Pipi and Kuku streets. The roads were unsealed and there were only two street lights . . . 'Only a small number of families actually lived there with some of the cottages for holidays and other areas vacant.' The first expansion took place in the 1950s when a row of about 30 small fishing cottages was built along the sea front north of the village. Most of these gradually turned into permanent residences in the late 1990s.

From the 1930s until the end of the 1960s, Te Awanga was a very popular holiday spot for Napier and Hastings families, many of whom owned basic little baches there. During the summer

OPPOSITE
Te Awanga.

holidays the whole family would settle in until it was time to go back to school.

Judy Lee, whose family had a bach with no bath or telephone, remembers: 'Te Awanga was a very busy little village in those days. The camping ground and every dwelling would be full – often as not with the same families every year. Activities at the camp would keep kids occupied for much of the day with competitions on the beach and races on the green and at night, movies from the back of a truck, concerts or talent quests . . . We spent all day and often evening, too, swimming, walking to Clifton or further to Rabbit Gully to see the glow-worms or to the Cape . . .'

In the early 1980s a much larger development took place when farmland on the west side of Clifton Road was subdivided into about 100 sections. Houses very quickly replaced bare paddocks. Today Te Awanga has a sizeable residential community, with many people commuting daily to work in the nearby towns of Havelock North, Hastings or Napier.

asking permission, Frank's brother-in-law Dudley Hill built three new huts or whare at the Cape. In Edward's view: '... it is coming it rather strong making a regular township on what he must know is an important sheep road and often a holding ground for us when driving.' Angered by people trespassing over Clifton shooting rabbits and goats, he put several adverts in the local press threatening prosecution, sent a chilly letter to a neighbour whose dogs had bailed up Clifton cattle, and grew increasingly disaffected with the golf club, disliking its factionalism. A leather company that he and Frank had invested in – to their cost – prompted more irate correspondence.

In addition to these varied irritants, Edward had to cope with a protracted drama involving a young cook, Fanny Hemmings, who developed a religious mania. He organised, with considerable care and sensitivity, her ensuing hospitalisation. Unfortunately, however, she returned to Clifton several times, and eventually wrote an abusive letter to Edward, who had at all times acted supportively towards her. By March 1910, he was urging Frank and Nelly to curtail plans for side-trips on the way home, adding: 'from a personal point of view I shall not be sorry to see you back here'. This was probably an understatement.

Frank and Nelly returned in time for the October shearing. In December 1910, Edward sailed home to Devon. A year later, Frank wrote to him advising that it was time to dissolve Gordon Brothers: by doing so, taxation on the divided property would be significantly less. Everything was in place for Haupouri to run as a separate

OPPOSITE
Vanquished prey in the front hall.

block. The official date for the division was 1 March 1912. The mortgages to the family, which amounted to £41,400 would be evenly divided between both properties.

Although Gordon Brothers ended £3000 in credit, that was quickly eaten up by building costs. Frank erected a new woolshed at the outstation and refitted Clifton's woolshed with Oregon pine. He built a cottage for Perry Wilder, who was to manage Haupouri on a salary of £150 per annum, and, when Wilder married at the end of the year, a house on the hill overlooking Whakapau Bluff. He also had various facilities erected at Haupouri, including a station cookhouse, a cart shed, and a storage shed. In 1912, getting in all of the stock to divide up and earmark was a major undertaking. Dipping, which normally took two weeks, ended up taking six because of this task. Frank started work at 4.30am and returned home around 8pm. The Clifton brand JGG over an anchor — remained the same; Edward's was now ERG over an anchor.

Today, the Clifton homestead is full of reminders of Edward's brief time at the station.

Edward never returned to New Zealand. Sadly he suffered a stroke not long after returning to England, and died, aged 50, in 1914. He bequeathed Haupouri in equal parts to Charlie's sons Mick, Pat and Ian, and to Lindsay. Perry Wilder capably managed the station until 1924, when Mick Gordon became manager. Today, the Clifton homestead is full of reminders of Edward's brief time at the station. His various hunting trophies still adorn the hall, along with his 9th Lancers' helmet; his service medals are displayed in a lined case on the Indian sideboard, and his photographs of officers who, like himself, served in the Relief of Kimberley, hang on the wall in the old office.

OPPOSITE
Edward's 9th Lancers' helmet displayed in the hall.

CHAPTER FOUR
TESTING TIMES

Clifton might have become physically smaller, but it continued to consume most of Frank Gordon's formidable energy. Now in his late forties, his schedule had become even more hectic, especially during mustering and shearing times, because his new role as chairman of the Hawke's Bay County Council ate up some three days a week. The weather caused the usual problems and farming worries. Writing to his father in June 1912, he complained: 'I don't think I can remember seeing less water than there is this year, all our swamps are still dry . . .' A few weeks later he reported: 'a very rough Sunday and Monday this week, a regular hurricane with snow, hail and thunderstorms all at once.'

Staffing and wage issues at the station also caused headaches. Labour relations throughout the country were particularly tumultuous at this time, with strikes and worker unrest increasing. In November 1912, after refusing to rehire a troublesome shearer, Frank was sued for breach of the shearers' award. He (and his farming neighbours) heaved a sigh of relief when the court found in his favour.

Despite these and other minor trials, life and work proceeded along a relatively smooth path. Sheep farming remained profitable. Frank and Nelly continued to enjoy outdoor recreations along with friends and family. They also took quiet pride in the children, who were growing up. Eileen, now an attractive, pleasant young woman, was seeing Dick St Hill, whose family owned a farm in Whangaehu. Lindsay surprised his parents by leaving school early and returning to New Zealand. He didn't stay long at Clifton, however, choosing instead to take up a cadetship at Edenham Station near Elsthorpe. Life seemed settled and proceeded along fairly predictable grooves. But testing times lay ahead.

'IN REVERENT SILENCE'

On 14 January 1913, Nelly was killed when a train crashed into the stalled car in which she was travelling near Kaukapakapa. She was 41. The driver, her brother-in-law Dudley Hill, and the other passenger, her sister Nina, survived without serious injury.

Light-hearted and kind, Nelly had been the perfect counterbalance to Frank's tendency to worry. Devoted to her family, she took great pleasure in the garden, dogs, horses and chickens, and specialised in hosting wonderful camping and picnic expeditions. The domestic staff at Clifton loved and respected her, as did the local community generally. The *Hawke's Bay Herald*'s account of her funeral on 18 January 1913 offers an insight into the scale of the sorrow following her death:

> *The cortege left the Hastings railway . . . and as it wended its way through the streets hundreds of people watched it pass in*

ABOVE
Family portrait: Lindsay, Nelly, Eileen and Frank Gordon, c. early 1900s.
GORDON FAMILY COLLECTION

ABOVE
Nelly on the west verandah at Clifton with her dogs.
GORDON FAMILY COLLECTION

reverent silence. No doubt the love and admiration felt for the late Mrs Gordon, as well as the universal popularity of Mr Gordon, contributed to the fact that the funeral was one of the largest, if not the largest, which has been seen in Hastings. When the hearse, heavily banked with the most beautiful wreaths, moved away from the station, it was followed by over fifty vehicles, and with others joining en route by the time the burial ground was reached the sad procession consisted of just on one hundred conveyances, each bearing its quota of friends, who had come from all parts of the district to pay tribute to the memory of the dead . . . The funeral passed along the Havelock road to the accompaniment of the muffled tolling of the bells from the Church of the Sacred Heart, and it was plainly evident that the awfulness of the tragedy had touched the people to the very heart.

For Frank, the grieving process was assisted by his strong sense of duty and capacity for work. Writing to his father following Nelly's death he explained how working on the station helped take his mind off his loss:

We received your message of sympathy for which the children and I are very grateful.

My correspondence has been very heavy this last week 181 letters in all to write thanking for 107 letters, 39 telegrams and 35 wreaths. I could not stand the idea of a formal printed card and it helps me along . . . I do not feel like meeting many people yet so just go over once a week to see the old people [Nelly's parents] and go to the cemetery which is close by. One thing that helps me along is that I can always find plenty of jobs to do . . .

TRIBULATION AND OPPORTUNITY

Frank could indeed take refuge in work, as there certainly was never a shortage of it to do at Clifton. It was soon dipping time, which meant a 3.30am start and long hours. The station was then very short-staffed, with only Frank, John Sommerville, and a boy doing all the mustering. Once Clifton's dipping was complete – a 10-day process – Frank began dipping for his neighbours on the Hamlin and Ruddick farms, which had 3704 and 2182 sheep, respectively.

The year 1913 continued to be an *annus horribilis*. Hawke's Bay suffered a major drought, with 10.43 inches (26.5 centimetres) of rain as opposed to 25 (63.5) the previous year. This caused much ongoing stress, although in the end Clifton still managed reasonable lambing percentages (85 per cent). In addition to the shortage of shepherds, the Clifton gardener was sentenced to a term in Napier prison for theft. Frank also found it hard to hire someone suitable to do more fencing on the Cape block. Then in November a general strike erupted, threatening meat and wool exports throughout the country. Farmers formed volunteer groups of mounted constabulary, as people (many from outside the union movement), both in Wellington and elsewhere, began to throw missiles and generally incite violence during strike protests. Frank, disgusted with these 'bands of hooligans' as he called them, would have volunteered himself, but was sorely needed at Clifton. Instead, Lindsay set off with his horse on the train and served as a special constable in Wellington for a time.

Frank, in addition to his other duties, turned his attention to shooting some of the 2000-odd rooks that were nesting at Fernhill and causing crop damage. He and the shepherds also tried to shoot as many of the wild goats roaming around Clifton as possible. (Despite their catholic tastes, these animals seemed to particularly enjoy new pasture.) Work seemed to be incessant, with not enough hours in the day. Frank's schedule was so exhausting that he decided not to seek re-election as county council chairman the following year.

Around this busy time an unexpected opportunity arose for Lindsay. Writing to his father, Frank explained the circumstances:

Rather odd, last night a land agent rang me up and I took it he said he had 5 acres, which was worth my while inspecting, so I said I would sleep over it. Lindsay was very keen to buy it and this morning I rang up and made an appointment and we went to see it.

On picking the agent up he said there is some mistake about the area, it is 580 acres, so in the blur of the telephone it was quite possible 5 acre [and] 580 to be confused. However I said it was out of the question but as it was handy we would go and have a look.

Upon doing so, Frank found the property, which was at Farndon, so attractive and the price so reasonable, that he put down a £500 deposit and procured it for Lindsay as a 21st birthday present. This easily-managed farm, although destined to play an important role in Lindsay's life, turned out to be something of a double-edged sword for Frank. Nevertheless it was definitely a bargain: a bright point in darkening times.

WAR YEARS

Frank responded to the outbreak of war in August 1914 with energetic activism. Determined to contribute to the war effort, but not from the Antipodes, he and Lindsay began making arrangements for a protracted stay in England. Reginald Pinckney, an attorney in Hastings who was Frank's trustee, would pay all of the station accounts and prepare the balance sheets. John Sommerville would

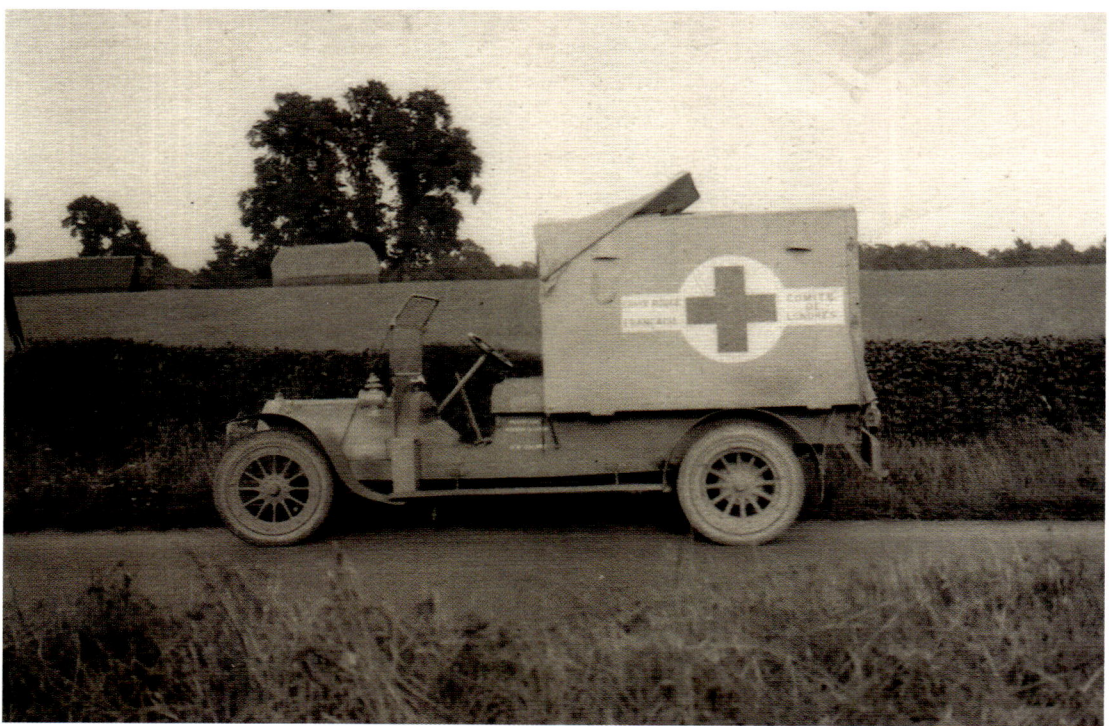

ABOVE
Lindsay's ambulance.
GORDON FAMILY COLLECTION

OPPOSITE
Three generations of Gordons, Devon, 1916.
GORDON FAMILY COLLECTION

manage Clifton. Eileen, recently married to Dick St Hill, was living on his farm in Whangaehu, so a housekeeper would take care of the homestead. Frank and Lindsay departed in late February 1915. After visiting Thomas in Porthill, Devon, they moved into Cluden House, Northam (which Thomas had built for his daughters Connie and Lizzie). Frank promptly bought a Bedford Buick to travel up to London where his services could be put to best use.

Writing to Pinckney in June 1915, he explained:

I have been pretty busy lately interesting myself in certain works, and the latest scheme is, I have an ambulance being fully equipped and as soon as it is ready in 2 or 3 weeks, Lindsay is to go over to France with it and then both he and the ambulance become the property of the authorities.

. . . This little episode will cost me £500 but it was the only way of his getting to the front quickly, and they are wanting help in this direction very badly.

. . . We are all awfully pleased that Lindsay is going as no young man can loaf about home who has any pride in him . . .

Lindsay served with distinction in France and Italy, and later, along with the other members of his ambulance crew, received the Croix de Guerre from the French government.

In London, Frank helped Lord Knutsford, chairman of the London Hospital, who was setting up two convalescent homes near London for soldiers suffering from nervous disorders. Charlie Gordon and Eileen, with Frank's persuasion, managed to raise £250 for this cause in New Zealand. In addition to helping Knutsford, Frank served long hours involved in other voluntary activities in London, most notably organising packages of dried food, shoes and clothing for soldiers on the front. He also visited all Hawke's Bay men wounded in the war, and wrote home to their families.

Although keen to return to Clifton, he remained in England. As he confided to Pinckney in February 1916:

It makes one wonder all the time, what to do, and when one is near and anything did happen to the boy one could perhaps be of help and if in the event of something happening and one had just gone, one could never forgive oneself.

Frank corresponded regularly with Pinckney, who was a trusted friend. He also occasionally wrote to John Sommerville, who had two sons serving abroad, and was looking after Clifton with his usual diligence. In July 1916, Frank wrote to him about a few labour issues encountered during shearing, concluding:

In any case please do not let these little items worry you, when we consider ourselves lucky we can get any work done, when you consider how things are at this end of the world. If you hear of any extra man of any sort . . . snap him up even though you make work for him and don't stick at a bit of extra wage.

With God's blessing and good luck wherever your boys are and with best wishes to you all at Clifton.

In a letter to Eileen the same month, he enthused: 'I was very pleased they had some wounded [to visit] at Clifton and when I write next I will tell them to do it occasionally and to provide for them as well.'

ABOVE
Best fleece
awards
certificate,
Panama Canal
Exposition,
1915.
GORDON FAMILY
COLLECTION

Sadly, the next news he received concerning Eileen was that her husband, Dick St Hill, had caught malaria at the Trentham Training Camp and died. Frank immediately decided to travel to Hawke's Bay and bring his grieving daughter back to England.

Unfortunately he never made the sailing, due to a recurring bout of debilitating neuritis, which had laid him low for several weeks the previous month. Weak and seriously ill, he hated being bedridden, complaining to Lindsay in a November letter that he was heartily sick of recuperating. Writing again to his son in mid-December, he kept him informed about affairs at Clifton:

> We had to give the shearers 25s per 100 this year and the rouseabout boys would not work for 1/3 per hour 2d an hour above the award rate so C. Tanner closed the shed down and sacked them. Sommerville and old Ebbett went over to Hastings and secured a mob and they only lost one day.
>
> We had 88% of lambs this year beating Haupouri and Taurapa.

I believe there is a great wool clip this year . . . they apparently had a very wet spring. Sommerville had plenty of help as Uncle Pat went over, Uncle C. Tanner bossing the shed and old Ebbett to help, so he should not have had too much to worry him.
With best love and tons of luck,
Ever your loving
Dad

The British government bought the entire wool clip that year, but Frank was concerned as it was taking them a long time to organise payment to the growers. Worrying about such matters, as well as about Lindsay, would not have helped his illness.

In January 1917, Eileen, accompanied by Charlie Gordon and his family, finally arrived in England. She and Frank moved to an Eastbourne hotel at the end of February, where Frank saw a doctor recommended by his London specialist. In March he wrote with relief to Pinckney that he had finally received the wool valuations: they would receive £5441, or £803 more than the previous year. By June, his health had improved significantly. Eileen began working in London at a servicemen's canteen, and Frank once again started putting in long hours preparing packages for servicemen. Writing to Pat Robertson in November 1917 from London, he observed: 'I am pretty busy here my hours from 9.30 to 7 most days and very little time to eat a sandwich.' To Pinckney in the same month he expanded:

My work here is increasing all the while and the standing orders for this month are about 160,000 bags. Luckily they have been coming in very fast and at intervals I was able to bale up all the regular orders as far on as to the 28th of this month some 40,000 in small lots, 10,000 go out to the British Red Cross every Monday and just as I was going to catch the train today an urgent message came for 3000 for NZ Hospitals and I just managed to get them together.

Some months prior to this, in July 1917, Frank had written to Mr McLean (a lawyer): 'Well! Dear Old Father has left us, which makes a great blank in the house.' Thomas Gordon passed away aged 90, having retained his vitality and enthusiasm for golf until near the end.

ABOVE
Frank and a shepherd taking a break.
GORDON FAMILY COLLECTION

After tidying up and paying off mortgages relating to Thomas's estate, Frank, who had worked so long and hard to make Clifton profitable, was somewhat strapped for money. Meanwhile Lindsay – who inherited money from Thomas's estate, and also had income from Haupouri and the Farndon farm – was very comfortably off.

Frank made a quick return trip to New Zealand at the end of 1917 to help sort out his own and the children's affairs, then sailed back to England. He, Lindsay and Eileen caught a boat back to New Zealand together at the end of 1919. In January 1920, in recognition of his tireless service during the First World War, Frank Lindsay Gordon was awarded an MBE. The medal is still displayed on the sideboard in the hall at Clifton.

NEW DIRECTIONS

Frank returned to Hawke's Bay after the First World War with both his children alive and in good health. This alone was cause to be grateful. Moreover, by arriving late in 1919, they had missed the terrible influenza epidemic that had ravaged New Zealand the previous year, taking 296 lives in Hawke's Bay alone. Adjusting to life at Clifton after almost five years away was not easy, however, for a number of reasons. Economically, the prosperous days of the early 1900s were over. Throughout the 1920s the state of the New Zealand economy fluctuated unpredictably. A short-lived post-war boom was followed by a sharp recession in 1921–22. It did not help matters that Frank's finances were somewhat strained, following Thomas's death, as he had to send money to England to pay off mortgage debts to his sisters and other relatives.

> **Economically, the prosperous days of the early 1900s were over. Throughout the 1920s the state of the New Zealand economy fluctuated unpredictably.**

In February 1921, writing to the Edinburgh firm handling his father's estate, he remarked on the lack of available credit from firms and banks at the time, observing stoically: 'I have been through tighter times than these before and it is only a matter of go a bit slow with working expenses.'

Other large-scale pastoralists were not able or willing to adapt and persevere. As the recession deepened, more estates were subdivided for sale or lease. In 1919 and again in 1929–30, for example, Karamu, the vast estate that had belonged to the once powerful, now-deceased JD Ormond, was subdivided for dairying, mixed farming and fruit-growing. The frozen meat industry struggled with rising production costs and falling export prices. Horticulturalists, many of whom had paid high prices for their land, also faced uneven or falling prices, although Hawke's Bay's pip-fruit industry continued to expand from the mid-1920s onwards. The quantity of fruit transported by rail from Hastings rose 76 per cent between 1924 and 1925, and by 140 per cent to 1932. By the 1930s Hawke's Bay was the second largest fruit-producing province in the country, with the highest average production per acre and the most modern equipment.

Times had certainly changed since Frank arrived at Clifton as an eager cadet in the 1880s, and not just in the agricultural sector. The old Victorian ideals and the small exclusive social circles of those days had given way to less strait-laced conventions and pastimes. This was the Jazz Age, with short-skirted short-haired flappers, and dance fads such as the Charleston. A new generation influenced by developments such as movies and radio, looked to America and Hollywood for inspiration. Interest and admiration for all things Californian was reflected in a new style of architecture: by the late 1920s Hawke's Bay boasted several white stucco buildings in the Spanish Mission style. Even parks and gardens began to have a more American feel, with date palms becoming a popular modern planting. Cars, the increasingly prevalent form of transport, helped transform the pace and nature of social contact. Local councils borrowed heavily to subsidise road construction and road sealing, electrical reticulation and other public works. A brief economic upturn in 1923–24 raised optimism for many towns struggling with debt, but the upturn did not last. The economy struggled on.

Cars, the increasingly prevalent form of transport, helped transform the pace and nature of social contact.

Frank, having spent the past few years in the centre of London busily involved in the war effort, must have found returning to daily life as a widowed sheep farmer in an economically struggling Hawke's Bay quite an adjustment. To add to his problems, the fact that his only son seemed to prefer the Farndon farm to Clifton became an increasing source of worry and disappointment. Lindsay spent less and less time at Clifton, although this was perhaps not surprising as he was courting an attractive, good-natured woman called Evelyn ('Ev') Allan, whose parents had a farm in Wairoa, some 130 kilometres away. Frank became increasingly disgruntled. His children believed he would benefit from marrying again, and if his new wife was comfortably off, all the better. They even went so far as to find someone in England whom they thought might be appropriate,

and persuaded Frank to travel there in May 1921 to meet her.

This scheme never eventuated, because during the journey to England, Frank became engaged. His new fiancée, Dorothy Halliday, an attractive 37-year-old, had just toured America and Australia with her starchy companion, Miss Wall. Upon arrival in England, Dorothy and Frank immediately went to Wiltshire to inform Dorothy's parents about the engagement. John Halliday, a wealthy merchant, his wife and their 11 children (including Dorothy) lived in an ivy-covered mansion. Dorothy's parents, quickly overcoming their reservations about the 19-year age gap and the fact that Frank lived on the other side of the world, bestowed their blessing on the proviso that Dorothy returned home frequently. The newlyweds honeymooned in England and Scotland, accompanied by Margaret, Dorothy's sister and closest friend. A talented water-colour artist with a gentle nature, she was a contrast to the more strong-willed, often tempestuous Dorothy.

When Frank, Dorothy and Miss Wall arrived in New Zealand in 1922, Lindsay and Ev, now his wife, met them in Wellington. During

ABOVE
Frank and Dorothy at their wedding, Salisbury Cathedral, 1922.
GORDON FAMILY COLLECTION

the long drive back to Hawke's Bay, Lindsay did his best to entertain the newcomers, telling stories and jokes, but his efforts met a chilly response from his new stepmother and her formidable companion. Dorothy's mood lifted somewhat upon seeing the Clifton homestead, which looked both imposing and very English, with its garden full of roses. Fortunately, too, Eileen's warm affection upon greeting her father helped to relieve the tension and lighten everyone's mood.

For some time, Eileen's diplomatic skills were heavily taxed, as Dorothy, feeling alienated in her new environment, sunk into a depression. 'Wall' (as Lindsay called her) did not help to ease his new stepmother's adjustment to life on a Hawke's Bay sheep farm, finding fault with all things New Zealand. Tensions heightened rather than diminished over the next few months. Eileen continued to run the household, while Frank worked long hours, and hoped his new wife would gradually come to appreciate life at Clifton. Lindsay and Ev eventually moved out, having purchased Farndon House located on the other side of the river from the Farndon woolshed. They lived there together happily, adding to and developing both the house and gardens over the years, and becoming popular, well-respected members of the local community.

Frank, disappointed by Lindsay's apparent lack of interest in Clifton, was at age 58, beginning to wonder about continuing with the large and physically demanding station. John Sommerville was on the verge of retirement, and in 1923 Eileen remarried and moved to Palmerston North. In August, however, Dorothy became pregnant. Turning her strong head for business to Frank's affairs, and with an eye to her impending child's interests, she focused attention on the Clifton inheritance, advising Frank to sell off the Cape block, and use the money to pay out Lindsay and Eileen. This would leave Clifton, some 2000 acres (810 hectares), for her child. She also suggested putting the homestead block on a separate title. She herself would then buy out Lindsay and Eileen's share of that. Lindsay ultimately thought these plans fair, but responded by saying he needed to consult first with Eileen.

On 5 April 1924, after a difficult pregnancy, Dorothy gave birth to a healthy boy, christened John. Frank now summoned his elder son for a decision about Clifton. He had hoped for a fight and was saddened that Lindsay opted instead to walk away without a protest.

Yet Lindsay, a wealthy man in his own right, neither wanted nor needed to spend his life as Frank had done, working the vast station only to pay much of its income to English relatives. The fact that Charlie's son Mick was taking over running Haupouri doubtless caused Frank some envy, but he now had his wife and his baby son's interests to consider. The sale of the Cape block proceeded.

SELLING THE CAPE BLOCK: SUMMERLEE

Selling the first major block of land to someone outside of the Gordon family was an emotional hurdle. Frank had, after all, spent over 40 years developing the Cape block from a fern- and pig-infested wilderness into a productive part of the station. He also felt some sense of failure, that the family property of 13,000 acres (5260 hectares) had been reduced to 2000 (810) under his management. Dorothy assured him that this was not the case. Due to him, the station had thrived and prospered, providing a livelihood for family members near and far. It was simply the right time to sell, especially now that John Sommerville was retiring and Frank was growing older. Managing the Cape block would challenge even a much younger man.

Hoping for like-minded neighbours, Frank and Dorothy advertised the property not only in New Zealand but also in British magazines such as *Country Life* and the *Field*. An Englishman, Colonel William Neilson, was interested enough to visit the property in early October 1924. By 13 October, the deal was done: he bought 5175 acres (2094 hectares) for £67,275; (some $4,882,788 in today's currency). Frank reduced the price by a pound an acre after Neilson complained that he had believed the gorges marked on the map were streams. He also left some £40,275 that Neilson owed on the sale as a mortgage, and also agreed to allow Neilson to use the Clifton woolshed, yards and dip until he could build his own.

The new owners re-named the Cape block Summerlee. By 1926 they had built Summerlee House, an attractive two-storey English-style homestead on Karaka Hill, with grand views overlooking the Clifton flats, Napier and the hinterland. Maude Neilson and Dorothy

OPPOSITE TOP
Cape block overlooking Ranga Ika.

OPPOSITE BOTTOM
Beach below the Cape block; the stock route at low tide.

soon became great friends. Frank and the Colonel had a more fraught relationship, their initial cordiality weakened by various financial issues and tensions concerning Summerlee's continuing use of Clifton's facilities. Eventually in 1935, the Colonel built his own woolshed below his house. When, in 1936, Frank donated the beachfront to the Crown for a camping ground, the Colonel worried that this would jeopardise his stock route. In fact he continued to bring his sheep along the beach for another 15 years.

By selling the Cape block, Frank could finally pay off his mortgages to his sisters. In a particularly honourable gesture, he took it upon himself to discharge all loans owed to his family and his father's estate by both Edward's and his own estate. As a result, the fraternal tables turned: Charlie had 6500 acres (2630 hectares), while Frank now had a smaller block than his brother. But for the first time since he had commenced farming in the 1880s, his land was unencumbered. The profits were finally his alone.

WORKING LIFE, THE GREAT DEPRESSION AND DISASTER

From 1924 until 1928, Frank kept a diary. This recorded the various tasks undertaken at Clifton on a daily or seasonal basis, from mustering, dipping, crutching, dagging, fencing, sowing paddocks, and attending sales, to hosting visitors, going to various social engagements, attending council and other meetings and trips, seeing to issues relating to hiring or losing staff, and occasionally, when it affected the station, the weather. Written in point form and never diverting into emotional territory, these diaries offer an insight into the varied routines and demands of the station, as this entry for February 1924 illustrates:

6th, I went to Stortford Lodge Sale. 7th. Holt's lorry brought 1500 feet of 6x1Rimu. 9th, David [Allan, head-shepherd] brought Go-Ahead ewes home. I started to mix dip. 11th, shepherd brought in Rough Block two-tooths. I went to Council Meeting. 12th . . . 14th, mustered Toi, Deep Creek and Round Hill ewes and lambs. I rode

ABOVE
The dipping gang, including Frank, second from right, c. 1920s.
GORDON FAMILY COLLECTION

around Rough Block, saw 52 two-tooths missed. 15th, mustered No.2 ewes and lambs home and drafted. 16th, David and I drafted old ewes for sale and dipped them. 22nd, We dipped 1700 lambs. 23rd, Four men took lambs [along beach] to Reef and Go-Ahead. 28th, Finished dipping. 29th, All rams put out.

In April and May 1924, Frank briefly notes, between various other matters, the birth and christening of his son John:

April 5th, I went to town to see Rainbow and Chambers re Rissington Bridge. 5th, Baby born about 2.30am. 10th, Johnson carting beach whare to David's [cottage on the right of the Clifton drive, coming in]. 11th, Atherton started to erect at David's. 12th, David and I sowing grass seed in Reef paddock. 24th, Started crutching. 29th, Did No. 1 and Rabbit gully ewes.

May 1st, Hoggets in about 9 o-clock. I went to the dam, shot nine ducks. 2nd, Finished crutching. Margaret and I went to races. 3rd, Heavy southerly came up. Frightened to send hoggets along beach.

12th. Council meeting. Started to wean calves. 20th, Shepherds brought weaner calves out of Toi Paddock into Long Paddock and driving them about to quieten them. David and Johnson finished lining one room at his house. 22nd. David and Johnson building bathroom. Shepherds walking calves up and down road to calm them, and rams on beach in afternoon. 24th. John christened.

Station life in the 1920s and 1930s continued as busy as ever. Dorothy, now enjoying her role as mistress of Clifton, gave Frank useful business advice. Although she could be difficult and did not suffer fools gladly, she had a keen aptitude for business and was always a devoted mother to John. Having a young son gave Frank a new interest and focus. He still worked hard, keeping the station and homestead neat and tidy, but he also found time to pass on his enjoyment of golf and horses to the young boy. The seasonal agricultural cycle gave his working life continuity, and, despite ups and downs, exporting wool still remained profitable. His brother Charlie and his family were close by, as were a circle of farming friends and neighbours.

In 1929, the economic downturn that had characterised much of

ABOVE
Dipping in the old swimdip at Clifton, c. 1920s.
GORDON FAMILY COLLECTION

the decade dramatically worsened. The Great Depression descended, gripping New Zealand, along with the rest of the developed world. Unemployment soared in town and country alike. In Hastings alone, by October 1929, there were 329 registered unemployed. Even those still employed struggled to support their families as wages fell. National income had fallen 40 per cent by the winter of 1932–33. In Hastings, where unemployment exceeded the national average, one soup kitchen served 25,000 meals between May and October 1932. Work schemes commenced across Hawke's Bay in the early 1930s, but their work was rarely productive. Government believed that relief efforts should be kept to a minimum to make workers find paid employment.

Many Hawke's Bay station owners carried such heavy burdens of debt that they just walked off their land, but others like Frank managed to survive the hard times. He doubtless felt seriously aggrieved, however, in 1936, when the Labour government brought in a Mortgagors and Leasees Rehabilitation Act. Under this legislation, Colonel Neilson was released from paying the outstanding principal on his mortgage – a sum equivalent to $1,852,572 in today's money.

Many Hawke's Bay station owners carried such heavy burdens of debt that they just walked off their land, but others like Frank managed to survive the hard times.

Legislation designed to halt the collapse of the rural sector lowered interest rates, offered subsidies, and abolished the graduated land tax, but hardly improved the situation for farmers due to new farm income and sales taxes. Cutting back expenditure helped many struggling farmers, and so too did the practice, initiated at Te Hoe station in the late 1920s, of using truck-mounted blowers to spread phosphate fertiliser. These trucks were a common sight across Hawke's Bay by the early 1930s.

In the midst of this increasingly bleak economic situation, the region experienced a lethal natural disaster, one Frank Gordon and his son John witnessed first-hand.

TUESDAY, 3 FEBRUARY 1931, 10.47AM

Frank and a few of his men were on the Clifton flats repairing a fence on the beach on 3 February 1931. John, then around seven, was watching and helping. At 10.47am a devastating earthquake struck Hawke's Bay. For the rest of his life, John vividly recalled the events of that morning.

It started with a sudden, incomprehensible noise. Clouds of dust rose from the cliffs; trees crashed down in the plantation behind the houses, and cracks opened up in the ground. To the horror of the little group on the beach, the seabed then rose, and the water retreated. One of the men yelled out, 'Oh my God – we're going to get a tidal wave, boss!' and began to run. Frank, holding John tightly, stayed where he was, saying. 'We'll never make it, boy.' Instead, they stood mesmerised, expecting the deadly wave to engulf them any second. The sea eventually rushed back, however, not as a wave, but as a river. Across the bay, clouds of smoke rose from the Napier foreshore.

> **It started with a sudden, incomprehensible noise. Clouds of dust rose from the cliffs; trees crashed down in the plantation behind the houses, and cracks opened up in the ground.**

When Frank deemed it safe, he and John moved towards the house. Dorothy ran out across the front paddock to meet them. Embracing Frank and exclaiming over and over 'Oh, my darling! Oh, my darling!' with hysterical relief, she then turned on him for bringing her to this awful place: 'Oh, what a terrible country, I hate it! I hate it!'

The homestead suffered relatively minor damage. The brick chimneys fell, a grandfather clock, formerly on the hall landing, lay face-down on the ground floor. Several fireplaces collapsed, and the house piles sunk under the billiard room. Instead of repairing all the fireplaces, formerly Clifton's sole source of heat, Dorothy paid for a new central-heating system. She also commenced a special project

OPPOSITE
The Caledonian Hotel (top) in Hastings Street, Napier, and the Masonic Hotel (bottom) in the aftermath of the 1931 earthquake.
GORDON FAMILY COLLECTION

in 1932, using the fallen chimney bricks to build a picturesque English-style brick wall garden in front of the back drive.

The damage and loss of life elsewhere throughout the region as a result of the two-and-a-half minute quake was horrendous: 256 people died and thousands more suffered injuries. Napier and Hastings' central business districts (CBD) were almost completely levelled. Coastal areas around Napier lifted 2 metres, transforming some 40 kilometres of seabed into dry land, and draining 2230 hectares of the Ahuriri Lagoon. Clifton and its inhabitants were fortunate to have emerged relatively unscathed from a quake that still ranks as New Zealand's worst natural disaster.

Reconstruction of Napier CBD began as early as April 1931, and before long it boasted more small-scale 'art deco' buildings than many other much larger cities worldwide. The Hastings rebuild took a little longer, partly because a decision had been made to allow temporary buildings to be put up, and, once back in business, occupants were understandably reluctant to tear them down. In 1932 Hastings led the way trying to boost locals' spirits with a Carnival Week, while the Hastings Women's League held 'Happy Afternoons' on Wednesdays in the Trade Hall. In 1933 the 'New Napier' Carnival celebrated the resilient town spirit with floats, displays and performances.

Despite this valiant and determined positivity, the economic situation remained highly problematic not just in quake-stricken Hawke's Bay but throughout the country. Disillusioned with the Forbes and Coates government, and sceptical about its ability to deal with deprivation and unemployment, voters wanted a change. In 1935, Michael Joseph Savage won a landslide election victory and formed New Zealand's first Labour government. The political and cultural climate had, in the first three decades of the twentieth century, altered irrevocably.

ABOVE
Frank Gordon reading in the garden – with Dorothy's wall behind him.
GORDON FAMILY COLLECTION

OPPOSITE
Dorothy's wall in the Clifton garden, made from chimney bricks that fell during the 1931 earthquake.

A LASTING LEGACY

In the course of a long farming career, Frank witnessed a great many transformations – among them mechanisation, refrigeration, cars, new roads, electricity and the creation of several much-needed local bridges. Napier and Hastings boasted a great many more amenities, from businesses, shops and theatres to schools, hospitals and parks than when he'd arrived in the region as a young man in the 1880s. Since that time, too, a vast array of previously unquestioned conventions and social beliefs had been overturned or undermined, a process greatly influenced by the tragic losses and social upheavals of the First World War.

Although he had accepted and adapted to this change, Frank still had some fairly rigorous sartorial standards, and was not the sort of person to quietly sit by and accept scruffiness. In June 1934, he made his presence felt at the annual meeting of the Hawke's Bay Agricultural and Pastoral Society, complaining that in horse events: 'many riders looked so slovenly they might just as well come out in

ABOVE
Clifton camping ground.
GORDON FAMILY COLLECTION

OPPOSITE
Boating club, Clifton camp.

their pyjamas'. Although this sally was greeted by laughter, members 'took a serious view of the situation', deciding that 'the rules in regard to dress should be strictly enforced'.

In 1936, Frank's health worsened. At this time he donated the land for what later became the Clifton camping ground to the Hawke's Bay County Council. This facility remains a popular holiday venue to this day. A year later (just after John left Clifton to continue his schooling at Harrow), Frank became gravely ill. He died in 1938, aged 72, and was buried beside his first wife, Nelly, in the family plot at the Havelock North Cemetery.

A pragmatic, hands-on farmer, he sustained and transformed the station, moving with the times and making significant changes to the property.

With the exception of the First World War, when he had moved to England for five years, Frank Gordon spent his entire adult life devoted to Clifton. A pragmatic, hands-on farmer, he sustained and transformed the station, moving with the times and making significant changes to the property – including providing his brothers with large blocks of their own and selling the Cape block – when necessary. In the end he made the right decisions, and, through hard work and perseverance, left a lasting legacy for future generations of the family.

OPPOSITE
Clifton camp.

CHAPTER FIVE
HALCYON YEARS

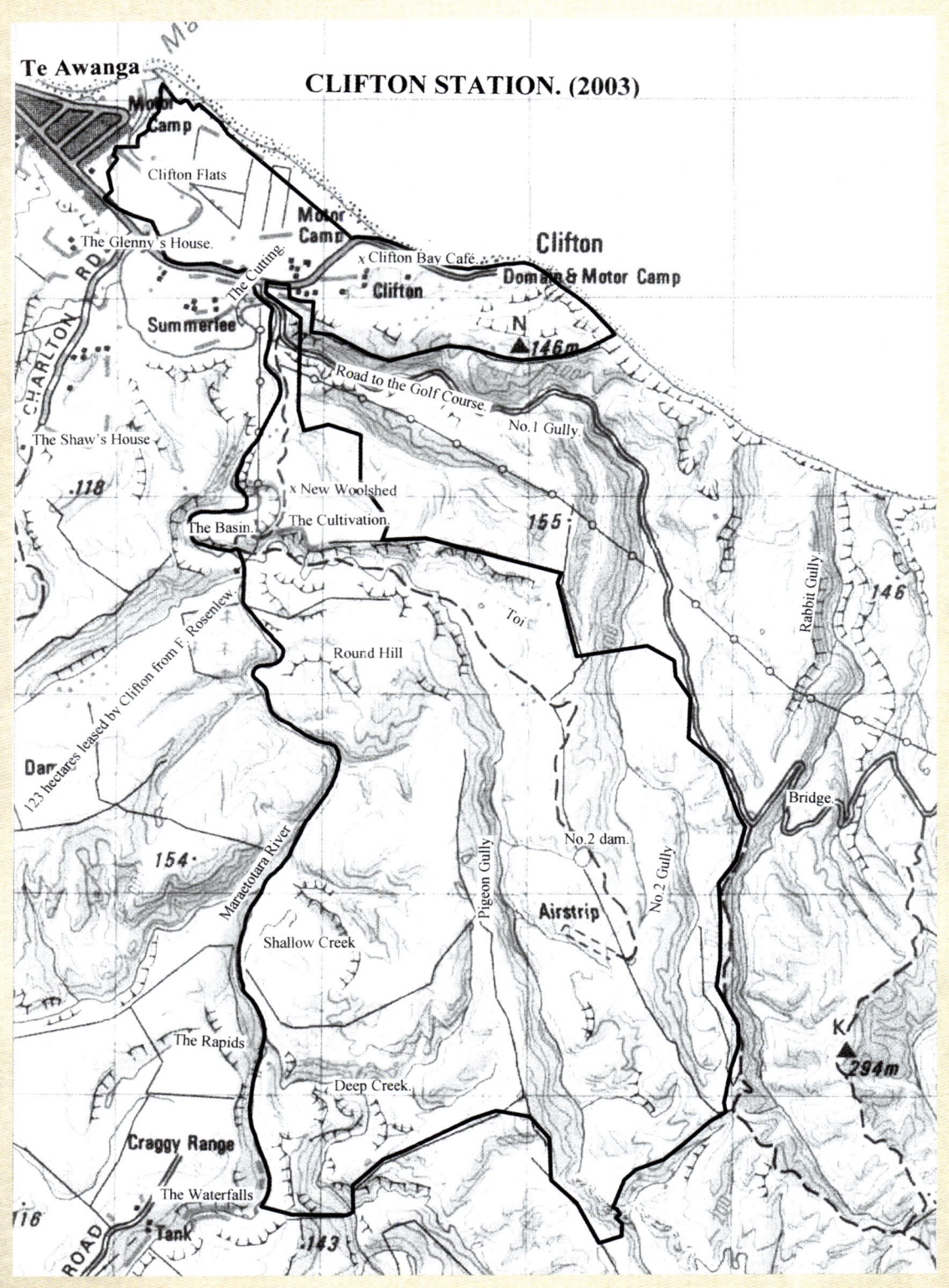

When Frank died, Dorothy decided to leave Clifton and return to England where John was attending school at Harrow. She closed up the house and appointed the Guardian Trust to oversee the station with Alec Law as manager. After four years at Harrow, John joined the army, went to Sandhurst for officer training, then spent the dying years of the Second World War with a peacekeeping force in northern Italy. He finally returned to Clifton in 1947. He found the farm slightly rundown, but quickly set about fixing that and resumed life in Hawke's Bay as though he'd never been away. Around this time, New Zealand began to enjoy a halcyon period of prosperity. Farming entered a golden era and wool prices had never been better. Over the next two decades, Clifton prospered. For John, these were busy, happy years.

Two permanent employees helped him on the farm: Frank Pulford, the general shepherd, and a cowman. In busy times such as docking or shearing, locals were called in to help. Frank Pulford left Clifton in 1955 to manage the neighbouring Shaw property. His replacement, Clarry Olsen, stayed on for 13 years, driving the bulldozers and maintaining fences, buildings and tracks. Over the next few years, several men and their families came and went, until 1972, when Lionel Wilkin and his family arrived from the Wairarapa and stayed for 22 years. Lionel had started shepherding as soon as he left school at 15, and, other than a break of a few years driving trucks for his brother-in-law, had spent his working life on various farms in the Wairarapa. He remembers how happy he and his family felt to be at Clifton: 'We came from a small place just north of Masterton called Mauriceville. We moved here [to Clifton] because

we just wanted to go back farming again . . . I had been farming and then had a break driving for my brother-in-law . . . and then Pat [his wife] had had enough of me doing those long hours . . . At first we never went away on holiday – we had everything here. You know, being close to the beach, we just loved it here, taking the kids down to the sea. The kids just loved it here, too. They reckoned it was the best time of their life.'

By that stage, Lionel was the only one doing the stock work with John, although he recalls they also had a 'fencer general who used to help at docking time.'

HOME LIFE

In 1949 John married 22-year-old Barbara Herrick. Her family lived in a big house called Lindisfarne (which subsequently became a boys' secondary school) just outside Hastings. The Herricks were friends of Frank and Dorothy's, for as Barbara observes: 'There were very few people in the area in those days, it was a very small society. Hastings

ABOVE LEFT
John on horseback.
GORDON FAMILY COLLECTION

ABOVE RIGHT
John and his mother, Dorothy.
GORDON FAMILY COLLECTION

OPPOSITE
John, Lindsay and Eileen boating in the Maraetotara; John Orsborn, John Gordon and Angus dipping sheep; Ready for docking.
GORDON FAMILY COLLECTION

was a small country town, so those from the same sort of farming background all knew each other.'

John and Barbara settled into the Clifton homestead, which Barbara warmed to from the outset: 'I grew up in a big house so it wasn't intimidating. The other house, Lindisfarne, where I was brought up was actually much bigger. I just loved Clifton from the moment I was there.'

Before the arrival of children, Barbara, who had always been a keen rider, spent many days out on the farm with John: 'I really loved it, riding out on the farm. It was lovely, and at lambing time I went to help. But about six months after I had been there I became pregnant,

TOP
Young Barbara on horseback.
GORDON FAMILY COLLECTION

BOTTOM
John and Barbara at the races.
GORDON FAMILY COLLECTION

ABOVE
John and
Barbara.
GORDON FAMILY
COLLECTION

so that was the end of that.'

John, effectively an only child, had always longed to have a sibling – even though he did have a half brother and half sister, 30 and 32 years older respectively – and was keen on starting a big family. Barbara recalls: 'We sort of set off to have children straight away. We filled the house with children, which was really nice, as the house lends itself to having lots of children. They made it come to life.'

Six children arrived in quick succession. The first was Angus born in 1950, followed by Jenny, Rosie, Edward, Serena and finally Charles, born in 1959. For Barbara these were busy years, running a large house, and organising all the children: 'We had a girl come in once a week to help with the heavy sorts of jobs, otherwise there was always housework to do. Washing day was a major event. We had an electric washing machine from the beginning, but had to wring everything through by hand. It took a very long time. Monday morning was entirely taken up with the washing of sheets – all the sheets were strung out on lines across the back lawn. Then we had somebody who came from Hastings on the bus and did the ironing on Tuesdays – she spent all day ironing.'

After several years, more help arrived in the form of two young Rarotongan women, Tapu and Rere, who lived in the house and helped with the children and cooking. Barbara remembers them as 'very congenial, happy-natured girls, who were wonderful with the children'. They stayed at Clifton for about seven years.

Barbara spent much time preparing meals: 'Breakfast – on the dot of 7am – was always cooked, not meat, but eggs of some sort.' Then part of the remaining morning hours were occupied getting lunch ready, as John generally came home, and there were often other men to feed, such as a stock agent, an extra hand, or visitors. Mutton dominated the menu: 'We really lived on mutton in those days. There was a sheep a week killed for the house and the cottages. They had either a forequarter or a hind quarter and we had a half a sheep a week for us. We never had lamb, only mutton. That half-sheep was made to last a week with roasts, chops, liver, and stews made of the neck chops and even brains.'

Lamb constituted a big treat, only enjoyed at Christmas. Barbara recalls: 'At Christmas time a lot of lambs were killed, which we gave to trades-people who had been good to John during the year. That was all distributed before Christmas, and everybody had lamb for Christmas so it was a real celebration of lamb. They were lambs that had been specially kept; ones that weren't good enough to go away, so they were kept and fattened up and killed at Christmas. Otherwise we never had lamb unless a lamb broke a leg or something like that, then we were allowed to have one!'

Nearly all of the vegetables were grown in the huge vegetable garden behind the house, or in the orchard down on the flats: 'We had a big vegetable garden, which the cowman/gardener looked after. And then gradually we had a

TOP
Rosie's christening.
GORDON FAMILY COLLECTION

MIDDLE
Angus's christening.
GORDON FAMILY COLLECTION

BOTTOM
The Gordon family, minus Charles.
GORDON FAMILY COLLECTION

TOP
A growing family at Charles's christening.
GORDON FAMILY COLLECTION

BOTTOM
Father and son, John and Angus.
GORDON FAMILY COLLECTION

proper gardener, so there was always plenty of vegetables. The gardener lived in one of the cottages, and whenever he was needed for something else – at shearing time or docking or something like that – he was taken away to help. When we first went to Clifton we had our own cows, so the cow boy came up and separated the cream and the milk in what is now the gardener's shed – that was the dairy shed. We had masses of cream, absolutely masses. That lasted for about six years, and then, when we gave up the cows, we used to take the cans over to Clive and get them filled up . . . They had beautiful cream and everybody had cream for everything . . . Eventually that all changed and we got pasteurised milk delivered.'

Anything that couldn't be grown on the farm was either bought in town at Williams and Kettle during the weekly visit into town or delivered: 'We would ring and get deliveries from Williams and Kettle, a stock and station agent that also had a grocery shop in Hastings. We used to buy sugar by the sugar bag and flour by the sugar bag . . . It was very good.'

ENDLESS SUMMER – A CHILDREN'S PARADISE

Angus Gordon has fond memories of growing up at Clifton. For him, as for his brothers and sisters, it was: 'a wonderful place . . . as close to paradise as it could be possible to achieve. We were spoilt for choices when it came to swimming during the seemingly endless summers – both the sea and the river being benign, but exciting. There were rides on our ponies behind Dad as he went about his mustering . . . trips out through Summerlee (now Cape Kidnappers Station) between Christmas and New Year to camp . . . picnics to the rapids and waterfalls at the back of the farm. Here, we could slide down the waterslides on sacks, pull enormous eels out of the deep pools, or lie in the sun after the picnic lunch presided over by Mum.'

Riding was one of the Gordon children's favourite pastimes. Charles, the youngest child, recalls many happy hours on horseback: 'Serena and I had a blissful time, as we both loved riding and had a variety of fabulous ponies, some which were bred on the property. We would ride to our friends Andrew and Felicity Casely and stay the night, or they would ride over to us and stay. Our favourite games were

TOP
John and Angus on the tractor.
GORDON FAMILY COLLECTION

MIDDLE
Picnic at the falls.
GORDON FAMILY COLLECTION

BOTTOM
Charles sliding on the falls.
GORDON FAMILY COLLECTION

OPPOSITE
The rapids on the Maraetotara River (which runs through the farm).

cowboys and Indians on the ponies all over the farm, through the rivers, round the beach to the Cape, wherever we wanted to go.'

May holidays were taken up with hunting, when the ponies were packed into 'Bluebird', the old blue horse truck, and Barbara drove first Angus and Jenny, and then later Serena and Charles, all over Hawke's Bay to various hunts. She remembers the challenge of driving Bluebird: 'It was an army V8 truck that had been used during the war and you had to double-declutch.' Serena recalls: 'I spent many May holidays hunting with Mum in the old truck. There were always heaps of kids, Oreka, Springvale, Okawa. It was all soft country. Mum and I and Charles would go off together in the blue truck; we would often break down, or sometimes we didn't even leave home because we couldn't start it. When we really hunted, though, it was great fun, especially when you had a good horse that could run and would jump anything anywhere. There was always strict protocol, you got into real trouble if you went past the [hunt] master.'

The children spent most of summer either swimming in the sea or playing tennis. Indeed much of rural Hawke's Bay social life, as

ABOVE
Barbara and Serena with mare and foal.
GORDON FAMILY COLLECTION

ABOVE

Angus and Jenny hunting.
GORDON FAMILY COLLECTION

Barbara recalls, seemed to revolve around a tennis court: 'It was a wonderful source of entertainment for everybody, because you had a lot of friends to play and it was great. It was also an intergenerational activity. We used to play a lot when I was growing up, we had a court at Lindisfarne, and then when our children got old enough, John and I had a court built at Clifton. It was wonderful. Tennis was very important at Clifton: one of our biggest forms of entertaining.' (A tennis court from earlier days, on the side lawn, fell into disuse when Dorothy installed the wall garden, taking up part of the court.) 'Families would come on Sundays, straight after lunch for the whole afternoon, or we would go as a family to other people's places to play tennis, have tea, a drink, and then home again. Sometimes we would go over to Taurapa and play tennis and have lunch, and also to Haupouri. Ian's second wife, Betty, was very keen about tennis, so we used to go there a lot when she came to live at Haupouri.'

During the school holidays, when the children were home from boarding school, they helped with lambing, mustering, docking and dipping. As Angus recalls: 'The holidays always seemed to coincide

Horses

Horses have always been an integral part of Clifton. Frank was a keen horseman and he, his first wife, Nelly, and their daughter, Eileen, were enthusiastic recreational riders. All the stock work was done with horses, as without them access to the backcountry was impossible.

Lionel Wilkin arrived at Clifton in 1972 with his own three horses: 'I brought three horses up when I came from the Wairarapa, which I didn't really need as there were always so many horses here.'

Barbara remembers that when she arrived at Clifton 'there were a lot of horses. The stables were on the roadside because there wasn't a road through originally. We had a stallion for the first six or eight years I was there. Think of all the horses that were needed on the station in those

ABOVE
Nelly and Eileen.
GORDON FAMILY COLLECTION

OPPOSITE LEFT
Angus and Dinah's daughter, Abby.
GORDON FAMILY COLLECTION

OPPOSITE RIGHT
Frank and a young horse and mother.
GORDON FAMILY COLLECTION

days, so all the stations had their own stallions.'

Barbara brought her own horse with her from Lindisfarne. 'The shepherds and John all had at least two horses, then there were the spares, and, when the children started riding, more and more ponies were bought.'

In the late 1950s Sarah Glenny, who lived on the hill overlooking Te Awanga, started a pony club at Clifton, and Barbara became a junior instructor. 'It took place down in the paddock below the woolshed. The other kids came from round about – quite a lot of children came from Tuki Tuki. Many started riding in Te Awanga because of the pony club. Many of them had never ridden before, so it was a pretty junior pony club. Pony clubs always waxed and waned, and ours waned as children gave up riding or went to boarding school so we joined up with the Tuki Tuki club.'

When the new generation took over Clifton in the 1980s, Dinah, Angus's wife, was instrumental in resurrecting the pony club. At first it was on Bill Shaw's neighbouring property, before moving to Clifton. It was very popular, and Dinah recalls that 'all the little local kids came with their little fat Thelwell ponies, and the average age of each pony was about 20 years! They were mostly from Haumoana or Te Awanga.

We had a fantastic district commissioner, Margaret McLean, who sent out instructors . . . I was involved for about 10 years.'

It was a strong club, with about 30 members. Gymkhanas, one-day events and hunts were organised. 'We had our own cross-country course . . . it was a huge amount of organisation . . . About 200 kids would come – it was a very popular new venue, they all streamed out here. We built the course in about 1994 when Ted was here. We did about three one-day events, and we would have had a gymkhana every year for about seven or eight years. Everyone pitched in and helped. Everyone in Hawke's Bay is very generous with their help.'

As had happened in Barbara's time, however, the pony club eventually faded away when it became more and more difficult to find good instructors. Over time, as motorbikes and then four-wheelers were introduced on the station, horses started to be phased out, except for recreational riding.

ABOVE
Dinah Gordon and Charlotte Fisher.
GORDON FAMILY COLLECTION

OPPOSITE TOP
Rosie, Angus and Jenny.
GORDON FAMILY COLLECTION

OPPOSITE BOTTOM
Serena White (née Gordon), Angus's sister, competing in Australia where she lives.
WHITE FAMILY COLLECTION

with docking, then the main shear and weaning time, followed by the dipping and hay-making in the early New Year. By the end of my school days, I had a sheepdog called Sam, and the holidays were spent working on Clifton with John Orsborn and Clarry Olsen, or on the new 750-acre (300-hectare) farm up the Maraetotara Valley called Otanui, that Dad had bought at the beginning of 1968 off his close friend Budge Poulton.'

This hands-on experience helped Angus develop the knowledge and skills needed to run the farm when he took it over in the early 1980s. When lambing and docking came around, every spare hand was roped in to help with both the mustering and docking. Barbara remembers: 'Lambing was a very important time for everybody. Angus and Jenny were a great help to their father because they could go mustering – they both loved it so, and it was really good. Rosie and Edward didn't ride at all, so they never had all that, and then Serena and Charles came along and they loved it, too. They also did all that lambing and riding, and we got more ponies as time went along.'

Riders or not, all the children were conscripted to help when docking came along. Edward, a non-rider, remembers: 'The highlight was definitely docking. Not being a rider I was always part of the late cavalry arriving by Land Rover to help with the final push to get the ewes and lambs into the yards. Having drafted off the lambs, we then dressed up in our docking gear, and I was one of the lamb-holders along with others. We all enjoyed the camaraderie and the humour, and although it was quite hard work it was great fun.'

Serena recalls: 'When it came to docking we would leave early in the morning to muster. We would get the sheep in from the hills on the horses, and then jump off as fast as possible, tie up the horses, get a large sheet and try to shepherd the sheep into the yards. Lambs were going everywhere, under the sheet, over the sheet, and our job was to get them back. Then the horses would pull and break bridles and then there would be horses loose. We kids would run around being shouted at by Dad – we were the dogs! There was chaos, and there would be a lot of yelling and carrying on. Everything had to be done so fast.'

After John bought the Otanui property in 1968, Lionel remembers how all the Gordon kids were carted up there to help out: 'When Fred, the manager there, saw, for the first time, John arriving for

OPPOSITE TOP
Frank Pulford and Lionel Wilkin.
GORDON FAMILY COLLECTION

OPPOSITE BOTTOM
Shearing time at the old woolshed.
GORDON FAMILY COLLECTION

docking with all the family he thought: What is happening here? Why are the kids all here? But the answer was soon clear when they were all spread out to work – and when the kids weren't there, other people had to be found.'

Lambing was a busy time: rounds had to be made each day to make sure all was going well. Initially the flock was crossed with English Leicesters, which, according to Lionel, seemed to create extra problems: 'We used to lamb the two-tooths on the flats and we used to lamb just about every one, which created problems when I took them out on the hills the second year. They did the same and would walk off and leave their lambs, the woolshed was just about full trying to keep mother lambs on.'

In time, though, the breed of preferred sheep gradually changed to open-faced, easy-care Romneys: 'We started buying different rams, easy-care rams. It made a huge difference to the mustering. They seemed to run freer. It took about two years to get them right, but it made a huge difference to the lambing also. The percentages were going up a bit, and a lot less work. Then we started the policy that if a ewe didn't bring a lamb to the docking board I tagged it, and if it did the same next year it was culled out. So we got much higher percentages and not so many deaths through lambing troubles. It was much easier to go around.'

Mustering for shearing was a major job. As Barbara points out: 'Don't forget all those things were so slow. Nothing was mechanised and everything took days to do, like getting the sheep

OPPOSITE
The old woolshed.

in from the back of the farm. They all had to come through on the road to the woolshed. All that took days.'

Up until the mid-1980s there was only one shear a year, at the beginning of November. Lionel remembers that, 'we were shearing about 3200 ewes and about the same number of lambs, so about 6400 sheep to shear. Mustering always started early. We saddled up and left at about 4 or 5am, because by the time you got out to the back it was over an hour's ride. We used to start out about four or five days before the shearing began.'

The sheep were mustered from their various paddocks, then brought down as one mob through the cutting, onto the road and into the yards: 'It was a performance. There were no fences and they would go up over the ridge, and if a lamb was breaking they would be all over the show.' Angus agrees that 'It was a very tense time, with a lot of shouting!'

> **'Māori shearers all coming over from the whare, singing all the way over, the whole shed was just music – the humming of the machinery, the singing, the swishing of the broom.'**

The shearing gang would arrive and move into the whare (shearers' quarters). Barbara recalls: 'There seemed to be masses of people – cooks, rousies, shearers, wives, children and a few hangers-on. We supplied them with meat from the farm – a sheep was always killed for them – and they did their own cooking.'

Serena's childhood memories include: 'Māori shearers all coming over from the whare, singing all the way over, the whole shed was just music – the humming of the machinery, the singing, the swishing of the broom. It was such a tight system everybody in sync. Dad out the back getting the sheep in, then everything would stop and go silent and we would have smoko. And then off we would go again. The Māori girls were the rousies, they chucked the whole fleeces onto the table, cleaned off the dirty wool and then a wool-classer checked it.'

For many years, until the early 1970s, Charlie Gillies and his

OPPOSITE
Shearing.

gang came and set up home in the whare. After his death, however, shearing gangs no longer came to stay but instead came out from Hastings by the day.

BOOM TIMES FOR FARMING

Throughout the 1950s and 1960s New Zealand enjoyed one of the highest living standards in the world. The Korean War 1950–53 created a wool boom, as the Americans started to stockpile wool in case of a prolonged war. Consequently wool prices rose 130 per cent almost overnight. The whole farming sector enjoyed a period of prosperity at this time, thanks to technical and mechanical developments, and to aerial top-dressing, which increased the land's stock carrying capacity and allowed previously uneconomic areas to be farmed.

Clifton, too, benefited from such innovations, particularly top-dressing. To maximise stock carrying capacity, each year large quantities of super-phosphate were dropped all over the farm. In the 1950s, John and the shepherd Frank Pulford built an airstrip right at the back of the farm, from which it was cheaper and easier to top-dress the whole property.

In the early 1980s, for example, 1500 tons of lime was carted out to the strip over a three-week period, and dumped from a Fletcher plane at the rate of 1 ton to the acre over all the steep country. Angus observes: 'The pilot, Bernie Symonds, claimed that he must have created some sort of a record when he put on 288 tons in one day. The plane took a ton each time. It was an impressive sight, seeing a procession of trucks crawling along the 3-mile rough farm track from dawn to dusk just to keep up with him.'

New Zealand farming throughout this period also enjoyed substantial subsidies. Since the mid-1960s these had increased from just 3 per cent of farm income to nearly 40 per cent in 1984 in the sheep sector alone. A supplementary minimum price scheme (SMPs) introduced in 1978 guaranteed farmers a stable income despite falling world agricultural prices. At the same time, various other assistance was also readily available – concessionary livestock valuation schemes, fertiliser subsidies, cheap loans, lucrative incentives for land development, and ample tax rebates. Until the early 1980s, even though farming Clifton was hard work, because of rugged land conditions, the station could continue to be farmed traditionally while providing the family with a good living.

Dogs

Without dogs, backcountry farming would have been well-nigh impossible. Everybody had a team of at least three or more dogs. John had at least six, because, as Lionel observes, 'Clifton was a tough place for dogs really. On that shingle and up and down those steep hillsides, their feet got very sore, so spares were needed. You worked your dogs hard for three or four days, and then they would be tied up for a week or so, and when you let them off again they would want to get back into work.'

The shepherds all had their own teams of dogs. Lionel arrived at Clifton with a lot of dogs because, as he explained, 'I did a lot of mustering by myself, and because of the tough country they would rip their pads off so you needed spares.'

Old sheep were kept for dog tucker, so

ABOVE
Dogs Storm and Grizz in the Can-Am.

OPPOSITE
Angus and his dog Grizz.

whenever the killing was done the dog tucker was done at the same time. Barbara recalls, 'There was a little safe down at the killing shed, and it was all hung in there, all very neat and free from flies. Because of hydatids, no internal organs were ever given to dogs in those days, unless it was all boiled up first. So there was a huge boiler next to the killing shed into which hearts, livers, kidneys and the like were thrown, and then boiled into a grey-looking mess which the dogs loved.'

Life for the dogs improved when four-wheel-drives were introduced. 'The dogs loved the four-wheel-drives. That was better for them because they didn't have that long run on the very stony ground to get to the back of the farm; and because they were on the motorbikes they were all fresh to do their mustering.'

Dogs remain an important component of farming Clifton. As Angus explains: 'Dogs are vital. We wouldn't be able to run the farm without them. We have mainly huntaways now, as we move a lot of cows and lambs need pushing a lot. I have two huntaways, Storm and Grizz, and Tom has two called Bounce and Ruff. He also has a heading dog called Tink. We buy them for around $1500 to $3000 each from people who breed and train them.'

DROUGHTS AND FLOODS

It was not all plain sailing, however. In 1973, Lionel's second year at Clifton, a major drought occurred. There was no grass and the cattle were grazed along the roadside. 'We hired a young lad [to look after them], and we used to have cattle grazing all the beachfront all the way to Haumoana and down at Mangaterere [near Havelock North]. Then when that grass ran out, they were trucked to different places around the North Island to graze – to Whangaehu near Whanganui, the weaners to Putaruru, in the central North Island, and to Frasertown in Wairoa. This latter destination ended in disaster. Despite plenty of assurances to the contrary, the farmer there neglected them, and did not move them onto new pastures. Of the 250-strong mob sent to Wairoa, 30 starved to death and the rest very nearly did, returning to Clifton as just skin and bone.'

Then the next year there was a 'one in a hundred year flood'. John and Barbara had gone to Europe, leaving Lionel in charge. On the evening of 15 June, after 45 centimetres of heavy rain, the river burst its banks, taking everybody completely by surprise. Lionel vividly recalls that night: 'We came home probably about 9 o'clock, and about an hour later Tom Butler, the fencer, rang. He was stuck on the bridge and said, "I can't get home – the water's got me . . . All my four children are at home in the cottage." Pat and I got in the Land Rover to go and rescue him. We had just got to the Summerlee gate and there was a roar of water and it just about took the Land Rover on its side . . .'

They couldn't get through, so had to return home.

The devastation was the worst in living memory. 'I had put sheep in the top river-bed paddock that day, and I brought them up and put them in the laneway thinking they would be safe, but they drowned in there because the river came through the cutting. It just roared through there. The bulls on the flats got stuck in the swamp paddock and they got in behind the plantation, on a small island of higher ground, the trees must have helped them. Some of the horses got in there as well. It was all dark, we couldn't see a thing. It was a nightmare. We went home. There was nothing we could do.'

By the time Pat and Lionel reached home, the power and phones had gone and would remain off for the next four days. Just after they returned home, there was a knock on the door and a drenched camp

caretaker came in asking to use the phone, because an old man living in the house at the end of the beach had died of a heart attack. Lionel remembers: 'Nothing could be done. He had to stay there for over a day until the fire brigade could get the grader through – they came through and got his body and took it out on the grader.'

> **The flats were a sea of water, all the fences had been buried by silt or ripped out, the floodgates had vanished, and there was no drinking water on the place because all the pumps were submerged under water.**

The next morning in the light of day, the extent of the devastation became apparent. The flats were a sea of water, all the fences had been buried by silt or ripped out, the floodgates had vanished, and there was no drinking water on the place because all the pumps were submerged under water. The hill behind the houses had numerous slips, trees had been ripped out by their roots and were lying across the roads, and in the paddocks lay large logs that had been washed down the river. Dead sheep had either been washed out to sea or were lying in pools of water. Although over 200 sheep drowned, all the cattle, horses and pigs survived. It took another couple of days to get out to the back of the farm to find out what had happened there. The destruction was immense. The roads were all washed out, the floodgates had all gone, and nearly all the fences had disappeared. Lionel recalls, 'There wasn't one paddock that I could say was stock-proof on the whole station, only the Cultivation.'

Lionel's first priority was securing the boundary fences, so he and several helpers set off to put temporary fencing on the boundaries to stop the stock getting out. 'The roads were completely washed out, so we couldn't get the Land Rover out there.'

Lewis Nicol and his bulldozer were called in to help. Once temporary boundary fences were erected, the clean-up started. First, they had to get rid of all the dead sheep: 'We had trailer-loads of dead sheep. They were so heavy because they were all covered in silt. We used to pile them up on the trailer, and we would take them down and bury them. But it wasn't only our sheep. There had been a lot of sheep washed down for miles up the river and stuck in the silt.'

Many sheep had also been washed out to sea and for the next few weeks they would wash up along the beach. Next, Lionel and his helpers turned their attention to clearing the paddocks of silt, logs and trees. Silt covered everything; there were piles of it almost 2 metres high in some places. 'We just had to pull it all out with bulldozers and front-end loaders. We got into it quickly, and that sort of stuff cleaned up quite quickly, but it was the fences that took a long time.'

Virtually the whole of Clifton had to be re-fenced – a long, slow job.

Clifton was without power for four days. Lionel recalls how difficult life was at this time for the 11 people in their three-bedroom cottage: 'We had nothing, we had the four kids from next door and our three children and my parents, and we all cooked on the fire until Tors, from the village – where they had power – brought us soups and all sorts of things. The village had all got together and got this food for us.'

The flood was a traumatic experience for Lionel: 'It took a long time to get over. Even after it was finished and we had straightened things out as much as we could, every time it rained I would be wide awake because it was a frightening thing.'

Despite his fears of another such catastrophe, he stayed on at Clifton for a further 21 years. And although nothing as catastrophic as the 1974 flood occurred, it was far from an uneventful time, with several droughts and all the usual problems of steep hill-country farming to contend with.

One year Lionel's horse dropped dead on a cliff edge, nearly taking Lionel over with her. 'John and I had ridden out into the morning and she had staggers (a sometimes fatal condition caused by eating too much rye grass). We rode out good as gold, and [John] went out one way and I went another. I got off to look over to make sure no sheep had gone over the edge, and I went to get back on and had just put one foot in the stirrup when she spun round and just went over the cliff. She was dead by the time she got to the bottom. Then I had to go down and take my saddle and that off. The staggers must have just come in while I was making sure all the sheep had come round underneath me. I had to walk all the way home and bring the bulldozer back to bury her.'

Another time he had to scramble up a cliff to escape a rampaging bull: 'One year we changed to the breed of Simmental. They were extremely wild and they would charge. One day a bull had gone through to Taurapa and I walked up the gully to see where he was. He came flying down after me, and I climbed up the papa bank trying to claw my way up and he was trying to get up after me. They were huge bulls. After a while he went back through the floodgate, I came back down and got back on my horse and raced off.'

THE QUESTION OF INHERITANCE

John had been the only child of a second marriage. His much older half-brother, Lindsay, and his half-sister, Eileen, neither of whom wanted to farm Clifton, had been paid out of the farm when the Cape block was sold in 1924. That left only John to inherit the property.

It was a completely different case for John and Barbara with their six children. Clifton was too small and not nearly productive enough to split six ways, so it was decided to leave the whole farm to Angus as the eldest son and find other ways of compensating the other five children. Barbara explains: 'As far as we were concerned, there was never any question of who would get the farm. Angus was the oldest and a boy, therefore he was going to inherit Clifton. Because of the size of the farm and because it was difficult land, it could never be divided.'

OPPOSITE
The Clifton flats.

Elaborating on this issue, Angus has observed that 'succession planning, as it is called these days, is always an important factor when you are dealing with a family farm. In the case of our big family, it was always going to be a challenge for Mum and Dad, especially if they wanted to keep Clifton in the family. Dad always knew what a hard, uncompromising block of land it is, and knew that it could only ever support one family without too much debt. Luckily for all of us, and particularly me, we had three amazing grandparents, who all paved the way for what turned out to be a seamless handover. Frank had done the most by hanging onto Clifton for all those years, even as he was providing for his family in England. He had made the painful decision to sell off the Cape block to help pay out his family as well as his son Lindsay, who didn't want to farm at Clifton. His second wife [Dorothy], Nangy to us, was a very astute businesswoman who had inherited money from her father, which she invested wisely. It was Nangy who bought Clifton House from Lindsay and Eileen . . . and it was she who set up an investment trust that kept Dad going all those years, living on the interest. It was with that money that the old man was able to buy Otanui farm, build the Kinloch house and buy more land at Lawn Road – all part of the succession plan. And finally it was Mum's father, Eddie Herrick, who was an extremely astute

businessman, who set up trusts, which enabled Mum to contribute quite substantially to the successful succession planning of Clifton by leaving her money to my three sisters.'

All of this planning and organisation has meant that Clifton has remained intact for future generations to enjoy. Angus, the fifth generation of Gordons to farm there, took over in the 1980s. He and his wife, Dinah, have kept an open home to his five siblings and their families, who have been able to continue to enjoy the beautiful family environment they grew up in. Lily, Jenny's youngest daughter, spent most of her school holidays at Clifton riding with Angus and Dinah's daughter Abby, while their respective brothers, Rupert and Tom, spent many holidays possum and goat shooting. Tom remembers: 'When he came down to stay we used to spend most nights out, we used to drag Dad out possum shooting out on the farm. We would go out right round the whole farm, we would usually get about 50 . . . Rup and I used to go chasing wild sheep, too, in the forest on bikes. We got 20 one year . . . And when we were older we used to go out goat shooting. It used to be so much fun.'

And now in 2016, the station is passing to the sixth generation of Gordons, as Tom gets ready to take over.

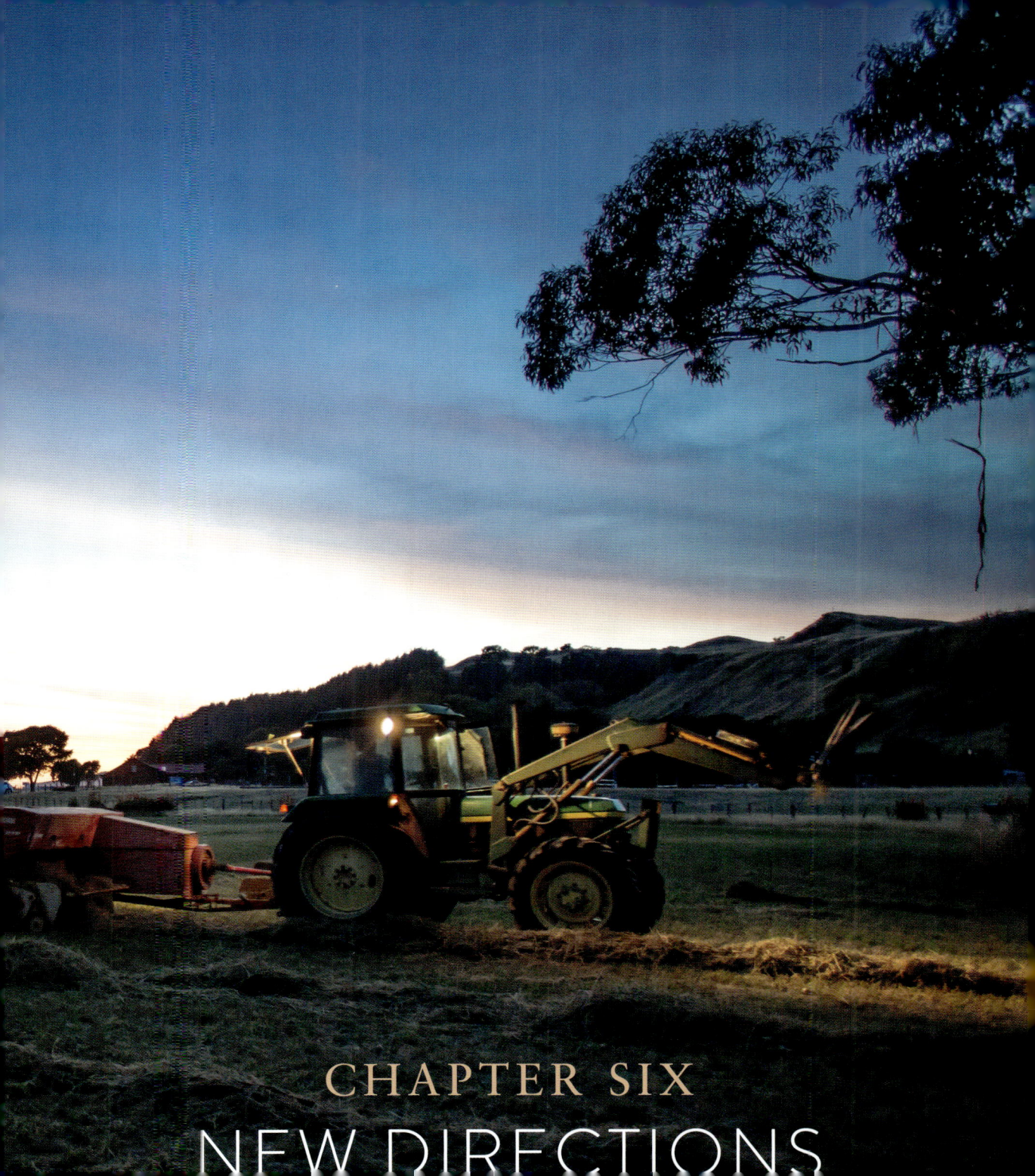

CHAPTER SIX
NEW DIRECTIONS

After several years away, first at university then travelling in Europe, Angus returned to the farm in 1977, just as the economic situation worsened. He remembers: 'It wasn't long before the hard times really kicked in: subsidies ended, wool prices crashed, and the debilitating droughts of the 1980s took their toll. The prospect of such a dry, steep, coastal block of farm being viable seemed very remote.'

Falling prices, the lifting of supplementary minimum prices (SMPs), the increasing use of synthetic fibres, and decreasing appetites for red meat all combined to make the next few decades extremely difficult. Wool, lamb and beef, the mainstay of Clifton for over 100 years, no longer provided a decent living. New income streams had to be found. But despite the enormous changes to farming and constant worries about whether a new scheme would make or lose money, family and social life continued much the same as it had done in previous generations. This meant riding, pony club, tennis parties and dances, and for the children a carefree existence playing in the garden or out on the farm with friends and cousins.

EARLY YEARS

Angus started working on the land he would eventually inherit feeling excited but also a bit wary: 'When Dad asked me to come home from England, I was very excited to be coming home, but dubious about how we could make Clifton viable because it was such a hard farm. However, because we had had such a lovely time being brought up

PREVIOUS SPREAD
Hay-making.

OPPOSITE
Tom mustering.

there as children, I always had a hankering to give it a go on Clifton.'

When he started work, Clifton was still a traditional sheep farm, with the bulk of its income derived from wool. It was thought that fattening stock was too difficult, as the land was so steep and dry. Consequently, Angus recalls, 'Every November the lambs would be weaned and sold at the saleyards to other farmers with better rainfall.' They finished them off for the works.

Calves, too, once weaned, were also sold off. 'We were a store farm rather than a fattening one. It was a breeding as opposed to a trading property, carrying 3500 ewes, 1500 ewe hoggets, 400 cows, 150 replacement heifers and 150 weaner heifers. Clifton then was predominantly a cross-bred wool-producing farm, selling a lot of its stock, including all the weaner steers on the store market.'

Angus and Lionel managed the day-to-day running of Clifton, while John concentrated his energies on an Aberdeen Angus stud he had started at Otanui, a good half-hour's drive away in the Maraetotara valley. Engrossed in this new project, he travelled the country buying bulls, attending all the national and local A and P

BELOW
Looking over the Cultivation and the new woolshed.

shows, and taking part in ward tours – organised by the Aberdeen Angus breeding society – to look at other studs both in New Zealand and overseas. Barbara recalls John's enthusiasm for this new project: 'He just loved it, it was a great interest for him. There was a much higher rainfall up at Otanui, so the pastures were much lusher. He could never have done it at Clifton.'

In 1989 John and Barbara moved out of Clifton homestead into Chicklade, the house John's mother Dorothy had built at Te Awanga in 1950. John, who had had a stroke in 1982, was then diagnosed with Lupus, a slow, degenerative blood disorder which would cause him a lot of trouble over the ensuing years. In June 1992, he was diagnosed with cancer and died in December of that year. His ashes were scattered from the top of Round Hill, the highest point on Clifton overlooking the whole farm and the bay. As Angus commented, 'I am in no doubt that he keeps a beady eye on proceedings and has plenty of comments to make on the running of the farm.'

Clifton County Cricket Club

In 1984, a group of old cricketing friends, Angus included, inaugurated the Clifton County Cricket Club (CCCC) in a paddock by the river on the Clifton flats. An AstroTurf wicket was laid and a small hut moved onto the property to be the pavilion. It was a hugely popular local family club and became an important part of the community, with whole families turning up to matches. The kids loved it, swimming in the river, playing cricket on the side, and sliding down the hills. Tom remembers: 'We used to play around and go down to the river, and steal beers and drink them beside the poplar trees.'

The CCCC visited other parts of New Zealand, and teams from various parts of the country came to play return matches. Edward, Angus's brother who

ABOVE
The cricket club today.

lived in Auckland, for example, brought a team down from Auckland for an annual match at which John Gordon and Pat Donnelly (a local farmer) were the umpires. After John died in 1992, Edward introduced the John Gordon Memorial Cup.

The social side was every bit as important as the cricket, as Dinah observes: 'There were some magnificent after-match parties, which were half the attraction for a lot of our members who weren't really cricketers.'

Christmas time was a major family event, with Father Christmas arriving in a helicopter or in Bill Shaw's plane or even on a bicycle. 'He would throw the sweets, and all the kids would rush about and get a present. It was huge fun.'

As the families grew up and moved onto other things, the club gradually faded out and became defunct in about 1997. Fifteen years on, it was regenerated by those who were the club members' children in the 1980s. Sam Howard, who was the driving force behind reviving the club, and whose father, Van, was one of the founders, says: 'I remember it fondly. They were all laymen cricketers, but they invited some amazing players down. [Former New Zealand captain] Geoff Howarth came . . . For all of us there was plenty of nostalgia over what were great days. So years later Matt [Nilsson, on whose property the club is now based] and I decided we wanted to recreate this for our kids.'

Within months they had 150 people wanting to join up, many of whom had the skills to help build the new ground. 'What we have now is a beautiful cricket ground . . . out the back of a farm . . . This is a cricketing community – built from scratch . . . with families gathering on the green and old mates catching up. Not all of our 200 family members are keen on cricket. Some are seven and just want to roll down a hill; others are over-the-hill and just want a beer!'

The club currently has 280 members, and the renewed CCCC has turned out to be more than just the families getting together on Sundays. The members are developing a youth programme and arrange games against local high schools. They bring kids out to the grounds, to teach

them to 'love the game . . . and take some advice from [former Black Cap and CCCC member] Mark Greatbatch'.

In 2015, during Art Deco Week, and while the ICC World Cup was on in Napier, a 'Legends of Cricket Art Deco Match' was organised. Some of cricket's past greats, such as Dion Nash, Jeff Thomson, Chris Harris and others, played against a CCCC team in front of a 5000-strong crowd. Now the club is also involved in planting trees for conservation and members are also working as part of the Cape-to-City predator-extermination programme. Despite all this extra activity, Sam emphasises that primarily they want 'the club to be something people truly feel part of, so that when new folk move to the area they are helped to settle, and that sense of community will drive the club for future generations'.

ABOVE
The original members of the cricket club.
GORDON FAMILY COLLECTION

ANGUS AND DINAH: FAMILY LIFE

On 21 February 1981, Angus married Dinah Eivers. Dinah's father, Bob, managed the huge 5600-hectare Ihungia Station near Te Puia Springs, north of Gisborne. There, with her four sisters and two brothers, Dinah experienced the sort of idyllic rural childhood the Gordon children had enjoyed: 'We rode horses and helped our dad on the farm. We spent most of our time out of the house doing things. We went out riding most days.'

When Dinah came to Clifton, she and Angus lived in one of the cottages before moving into the big house in 1989. Life was very busy: 'I did a bit of work for Mother Earth food company, distributing their products, a bit of apple-picking, a lot of gardening, and often rode out on the farm with Angus.'

She also went hunting in the season: 'I hunted when we were first married. Angus did, too. It was social and fun – everybody got to know everybody – but also serious hunting. It was great. I thoroughly enjoyed it.'

In November 1983, Dinah gave birth to a son, Tom, the first of the sixth generation of Gordons to be at Clifton. His sister, Abby, was born in September 1985. The next few years were a whirl of activity,

ABOVE
Angus and Dinah's wedding, with brothers Charles (end) and Edward (middle) as groomsmen.
GORDON FAMILY COLLECTION

OPPOSITE TOP
The homestead kitchen.

OPPOSITE BOTTOM
Angus's library.

punctuated in 1989 by the move into the big house. Dinah recalls those early days in the homestead: 'The difference was extraordinary. It was so much bigger after our little cottage, where everything was only a few steps away. But we were very happy to get there, it worked really well. The kids found it a bit daunting at first!'

Dinah's time was fully taken up running such a huge house and garden, with a little bit of help: 'We were lucky we had Jenny Napier in the garden, we couldn't have done it without help, it was so huge.'

TOUGH TIMES: THINKING LATERALLY

In 1982, John handed over the management of Clifton completely to Angus. Although Angus was thrilled to be in control, it was also the beginning of some of the toughest times Clifton had ever been through. The 1980s were punctuated by crippling droughts, collapsed wool prices, and changing government policies toward farmers.

ABOVE LEFT
Dinah, Tom, Abby and Angus.
GORDON FAMILY COLLECTION

ABOVE RIGHT
Dinah and Abby.
GORDON FAMILY COLLECTION

ABOVE
Angus and Tom. 'From when I was about two, I think, I went out on the farm with Dad. When I was little I used to go out in the box on the back of Dad's two-wheeler . . . It used to fall over sometimes, but they are quite light, they just fall over, and so I would just tumble out of the box!'
GORDON FAMILY COLLECTION

In 1984, the newly elected Labour government abolished all SMPs for beef, sheep meat, wool and dairy products. It also withdrew tax concessions for farmers, and eliminated free government services. By 1987, land development loans, fertiliser and irrigation subsidies and subsidised credit had also been phased out. The combined impact of this was catastrophic, particularly for sheep farmers. Some lost their farms, and those who didn't struggled to stay afloat. They had to think about ways to diversify and innovate in order to survive.

Angus, whose income relied on wool and lambs, was no exception. He has consequently spent almost his entire farming career creating new opportunities and finding new ways to make Clifton productive. His son, Tom, later observed: 'To make farming work here you have to think laterally. Dad has always done that and taken risks, but he's also kept in mind that he has to preserve the farm. So he hasn't been able to take huge risks, but he has done a lot to improve the farm situation and our family's situation. Doing the café was amazing, and that was a pretty big risk really, because at the time he had no experience in the hospitality industry – amazing 15 years later and it's still going.'

In 1983, one year after Angus took complete charge, a long and crippling drought set in. Dams dried up and the grass didn't grow. Once again cattle were grazed along the roadside between Te Awanga and Haumoana. Cow numbers dropped from 400 to 200, and hay had to be bought at inflated prices, pushing the farm into a precarious financial situation.

This financial situation was further exacerbated by a development project on the land in Mangateretere.

A winter drought in 1986 was just as terrible. The autumn rains never came, so, once again, the dams remained dry and the grass didn't grow. As a result, 350 ewes died of sleepy sickness – caused when ewes break down excessive amounts of fat to meet energy demands – and malnutrition, the lambing percentage plummeted, and the country, usually lush and green in winter, retained the parched brown bare look of summer.

In 1988, Angus leased 1000 acres (405 hectares) from his neighbour, Bill Shaw, just across the river. Thanks to this move, the 1989 drought, potentially the most crippling of all, hardly affected Clifton. Angus recalls: 'In 1988, I took on the lease of 1000 acres of

ABOVE
Angus and shepherd Tiki in the yards.
GORDON FAMILY COLLECTION

OPPOSITE
Dry flats.

Bill Shaw's farm across the river, which just saved our bacon going into the final, most devastating of all the droughts. The whole farm had a lot of old rank grass which proved a godsend for our cows.'

DIVERSIFICATION

Even before these bad years, Angus and John had looked at diversifying. In 1982, they decided to try fattening lambs on the flats. To do that, irrigation was needed. They bought a large Briggs irrigation system, but it proved very difficult to manage. Angus recalls: 'We had a lot of accidents with it, because it went round and round and hit the fences, and then it would go into a slip dip and the whole thing would go over.'

Lionel, too, remembers 'what hard work it was keeping it going . . . and then we found we couldn't keep up when it dried out even though the irrigation was putting on the equal of about 2 inches of water.'

Quite apart from these irrigation problems, fattening lambs over

ABOVE
Dry river-bed during summer.

summer was not a success because they got worms and flystrike and suffered from various other afflictions. Consequently that project was abandoned.

At the same time John, trying to make the final division of his assets more equitable, decided to develop a piece of land at Mangateretere. This land, close to Havelock North, had been bought many years earlier by Frank as a fattening block for Clifton.

Large amounts of money were borrowed to drain the land and install underground irrigation pipes. Angus observes of this scheme: 'We spent a fortune down at Lawn Road. We drained it all. We put tile drains in the whole of that land, and then brought an irrigation system in.'

They started growing beans and peas for Wattie's, which was very successful because it was possible to produce two crops a year. After a few years, however, Wattie's walked away from all the bean crops in the area as they had too much produce. The local growers took a case against them, but lost.

Angus and John then decided to plant 3 hectares of strawberries: 'We planted 8 acres of strawberries, which was huge, and we didn't know anything about it. By the time we got the strawberries, it was too late and we missed out on the export market. You could only export for one year, and then the next year they were only grown for process and there is no money in process. That was two years of back-breaking work.'

They started growing beans and peas for Wattie's, which was very successful because it was possible to produce two crops a year.

They ripped the strawberries out and decided to try nectarines because, Angus recalls, 'There was a big market for nectarines in Australia then. Unfortunately, by the time we had planted the nectarines everybody else had had the same idea and the bottom had fallen out of the market. We started harvesting them and realised it was costing us to harvest them, so we just walked away from that and then we pulled the trees out.' Not long after that the Mangateretere land was sold.

Pastoral farming continued to slump. Desperate to find a profitable alternative, in 1989 Angus started growing early squash for the Japanese market on fixed contract for John Bostock, a successful local exporter. 'By now the pastoral side of farming was at an all-time low. Clifton was getting between $4 and $10 for the old ewes, sometimes below $3 for a kilo of wool, about $17 for our best lambs, and $350 for our best weaners. I was game for anything! This seemed like at least an opportunity to try and control our own destiny. The 1990 squash crop was such a success that I was able to buy a new Ford station wagon, which we nicknamed the 'Squashmobile'. So each year we grew more and more squash; as the wool prices dropped to nothing, and lamb was hardly worth anything, we were very lucky that the squash took up the slack. We got up to about 120 acres. The whole thing about the squash for us was the fact that we were earlier than anyone else. We were on the first boats out of the country – it was very stressful – I went grey because every year I never knew if we were going to get on the first boat. If we missed the first boat the contract was null and void, and we went down to just normal price, which wasn't good enough for us. We had to have that premium on

ABOVE
The squash crop.
GORDON FAMILY COLLECTION

ABOVE
Angus and the squash ready for the packhouse.
GORDON FAMILY COLLECTION

the price. So as it turned out we never lost money on it.'

Thanks to the squash, the 1990s were relatively good years. So much so that in 1995 Angus decided to purchase 12 hectares of land in Vanuatu to grow squash. Unfortunately, after one successful season, the company he was growing for moved out. He then decided to plant onions instead. However, he recalls, 'They grew really well, and then at the last minute they all exploded – they had grown too big and fast.' Next he grew mahogany. The first trees were planted in 1997, and the last in 2004. Things progressed smoothly. 'The whole forest completely canopied over, we pruned the trees; it was beautiful and really growing well.' He expected to begin harvesting the trees in around 2027 – some 30 years from when the first trees were planted. Then in 2015, one of the most destructive cyclones Vanuatu has ever experienced raced through the islands, ripping up trees, destroying houses, and causing mayhem. On Angus's block, 'it ripped all the tops and foliage off the trees but left the bare trunks standing.' Luckily most of the damage wasn't irreversible: 'The trees have since started to regrow, although some trunks are now quite short and others are misshapen.'

Erosion

On the steep coastal hill country, erosion is a constant problem. After every heavy rain, there are slips that often block or destroy the roads and take out fences in their path. In 1973, a flood caused major erosion problems. Another one in 1992 caused more slipping and damage at the back of the farm.

In 2006, the house, which had stood in the same place for over 100 years, was nearly destroyed. It had been raining for several days,

ABOVE
A landslip behind the house.
JAN WHITE

which caused a massive slip behind the house. As Angus recalls: 'a great wall, like a glacier or terminal moraine, had come down, broke the gate off and hit the back of the house, then went down the side of the house in a river of mud about a metre thick'.

But that was just the last part of the slip. 'The big majority of the slip was just left in the paddock, it was about 2 metres high and it was just crawling forward like a lahar, you could see it moving forward very slowly . . . Looking out there it was like doomsday. There was mud everywhere, right through the trees as far as the eye could see, moving forward like a lava flow.'

Angus called his digger friend Merv, who came straight out. He scraped mud away from the house and managed to divert its flow. 'The majority of the material was just sitting up on the top of the hill waiting to slide . . . The whole thing was moving really slowly forward, you could actually see it moving – it went on for weeks. The noise was frightening at night. You would hear crashing as rocks came down and trees were ripped out, and you could hear big explosions as large rocks hit and smashed up. It was terrifying, but nothing could be done and no course of action could be decided on until it dried out.'

After a month or so, once the rains had stopped, consultants came out to inspect the scene and concluded that with another big rain the rest of the hill would slide, taking the house with it. They recommended that the house be moved. That was obviously not a possibility, so eventually it was decided to remove all the loose material from the top of the hill. There was an area of about 1 hectare, of 3-metre-deep loose soil, sitting on the clay pan just waiting to slide. So 46,000 cubic metres of soil were scraped off the top of the hill and taken down to the flats to build up a low-lying paddock by the sea: 'The whole process took about six months. They had trucks coming and going all day . . . and they just flattened it out and packed it down so that the paddock has now ended up above sea level and is a much safer paddock.'

In front of the house, erosion caused by the sea is ongoing. For many years it was stable, as large concrete blocks had been placed on the gravel to hold back the sea. However, in 2008, the sea started breaching the wall and eventually got in behind it. Then, in winter 2009, a huge storm destroyed most of the road into the camp. So Angus leased them some of the front paddock for their access, moved the fence back about 5 metres toward the house, and a new tar-seal road was built. Unfortunately at the same time the regional council decided to remove all of the concrete blocks that had been holding the sea at bay for so long, because they weren't particularly pleasing to the eye. Almost immediately the sea started eating away at the bank, and the new road was destroyed. Once again a new one was built, and once again it fell into the sea. Angus explains: 'We've moved the fence back four times, and lost between 20 and 30 metres of land in front of the house and café.'

Much of the camp has been wiped out. Where once there were 112 camp sites, there are now about 70. Finally the district council, who initially wanted nothing to do with the whole problem, changed their minds, and agreed, subject to resource consent, to put a rock wall right along the road. Hopefully that measure will stop the sea eating away at the land.

In 2010, 8 hectares of land had been leased to Elephant Hill, a local winery, and planted in very specialised vines. When the water hit, it 'came over the flats and hit the grapes, ripped them out of the ground, rolled them up into one great big pile of rubbish. The rest of the grapes were under about a metre of silt, so it would have killed them anyway.' As a result, the vineyard ended the contract to lease.

Then in 2011 the 'weather bomb' hit, devastating the whole farm. At the back of the farm, the fences were taken out, floodgates and tracks were destroyed, and hillsides slipped into the gullies. Tom, who had just arrived home from Japan witnessed it: 'The farm was a big mess from all the flooding. All the fences were broken and the hills had all slipped down . . . Brian [a friend] and I spent the whole summer fencing and fixing things up. It took about two to three years just chipping away at the fencing in between other jobs.'

Angus recalls that 'On the flats, water came down like a tsunami, a wall of water just took everything in its path.'

The huge seas created by Cyclone Pam in March 2015 did more

damage to the flats. The salt water killed off about 3 hectares of grassland. The sea crest has now moved about 10 metres into the paddock, effectively losing some 10 metres of good land.

Erosion either by the sea on the low-lying areas, or out on the steeper hills, is a serious ongoing problem. Angus and Tom do their best to combat it with plantings and by building banks, but this is not always successful: 'We are going to plant about 3 acres down by the river mouth as the sea is now coming right over the top and into paddocks. But it will be hard to get anything to grow in that environment as the ground is now so salty. Maybe sheoaks, which don't mind the salt air. We have planted comprehensively – eucalyptus, poplars, and some karaka and flax – in the big hole that was created in the 2011 weather bomb. And we have also planted poplars out on the farm, but they are unable to contain the big creeping slips we get.'

CLIFTON CAFÉ

For many years, Angus had been contemplating building a café close to the beach at Clifton. Tourism was growing exponentially in the area, with people visiting the gannet colony on the Cape, or just coming for a day's outing to enjoy the scenery. All the signs for success looked favourable. He recalls: 'In 1998, I decided to take the big risk and build a café down by the beach. And that's what we did. It opened in July 1999, and locals started pouring in and supporting it.'

After a fraught first two years, when Angus and Dinah were in charge – not something they had ever anticipated doing – Jo Logan and Sue Wylam, both professional restaurant people who had just sold their café Casa Gardini in Napier, agreed to come and run Clifton Café. Things immediately improved. Jo and Sue put efficient new systems in place, and the café started making money. Indeed at the end of the 2000 season, it won the Hawke's Bay Best Café award in the annual New Zealand-wide *Café Magazine* competition.

When Jo left in November 2001 to pursue a golfing career, Sue stepped in as front-of-house and manager, and for the next 10 years successfully ran the café. Business boomed. In addition to functioning as a café, it also became a popular function and wedding venue. In fact, Clifton Café was so much in demand that, in 2003, additions were carried out to accommodate greater numbers. Angus and Dinah were still actively involved. As Dinah remembers: 'We would go over and help. I used to do the menus and the computer, anything that needed to be put on the till, Sue was computer

OPPOSITE
Clifton Café.

OPPOSITE TOP
Aerial view of the café, house and hills with the camp in the background.
GORDON FAMILY COLLECTION

OPPOSITE BOTTOM
Café looking back to the old woolshed and farm sheds that the café was modelled on.
GORDON FAMILY COLLECTION

ABOVE
Sue and Dinah behind the bar in the café.
GORDON FAMILY COLLECTION

illiterate. I also helped in the bar or was the cashier person. I tried not to be a waitress and was hopeless as the coffee person. Once I had to be the chef – it was a very restricted menu that day! Angus did the grounds, the rubbish and the banking.'

When Sue left on Christmas Eve 2012, Angus and Dinah once again found themselves running the café – not a job they relished. Dinah took over for six months, a time she describes as 'terrible, a nightmare!' Angus, too, had to become actively involved, 'spending many hours there behind the bar – mainly washing glasses!'

By then, business had become tougher, with growing competition in the area, combined with the impact of the 2008 global financial crisis. As Angus recalls: 'It was very successful for a number of years. We reached our peak in about 2006, a lot of ups and downs, but very successful. In 2008, the global crash was definitely reflected in our figures. Also, by then the minimum wage was up to $13, and that suddenly made it more difficult. But we were still doing okay, just not the money we had been making up until 2008. Competition certainly increased. I would say that around Hawke's Bay, the number of cafés and wineries had probably more than doubled since we started.'

From the late 1990s, Hawke's Bay, along with the rest of New Zealand, experienced a huge growth in tourism. In 2000, cruise ships started visiting Napier in ever-increasing numbers. In 2007, 26 ships carrying 15,000 passengers visited. The number reached a peak in 2012 with 69 ships carrying 101,412 passengers. In 2015, 56 ships carrying 93,000 tourists visited Napier. The overall number of international visitors increased from 94,234 in 1997 to a high of 214,850 in 2015.

At the same time, growing numbers of locals visited facilities such as accommodation, restaurants, wineries, bike trails and rural walks. Art Deco Week, which started in February 1989 to celebrate the extraordinary concentration of art deco buildings built in Napier after the 1931 earthquake, attracted nearly 40,000 visitors, both national and international, in 2015. In 2014 alone, tourists spent $554 million in Hawke's Bay, with food and wine drawing in the crowds. More than 1000 people are currently employed in over 150 vineyards and 70 wineries throughout the region. Viticulture pours well over $100 million annually into the local economy, and tourism in the region contributes 6.5 per cent to the national gross domestic product. Visitors to Cape Kidnappers multiply each year: in 2012 numbers reached over 11,000. Many of these tourists went along the beach on old tractors, as part of the gannet tours run by Gannet Beach Adventures. Others travelled overland on the Gannet Safaris tour to see the bird colony. Angus's belief that building a café was a good idea has proved completely justified.

In 2012, Angus and Dinah leased the business out to Sue Robinson. After two-and-a-half years Sue and her husband left the area to work elsewhere, and Sudheesh Cheviri and Suresh Abraham took up the lease.

In the meantime, Angus had embarked on a new tourist venture in the old woolshed. In 2002, the owner of the Cape Kidnappers block, Julian Robertson, built a new Clifton woolshed 2 kilometres away from the main road towards the middle of the farm. This was necessary because Julian had replaced the old shingle track through the cutting with a two-lane sealed road, and traffic had increased enormously. This increase in traffic posed problems when mobs of sheep were being brought down to the yards near the beach.

ABOVE
The new woolshed with round hill in the distance.

TOURISM IN THE OLD WOOLSHED

The old woolshed has been turned into a museum and farm show venue. Angus and his partner in the new business, Ian Richardson (who had previously run a similar enterprise in Napier), rearranged the woolshed, built a stage and a small shop at the end of the shed, and set up a small museum. Farm shows commence with Ian or Tom showing visitors how his dogs work sheep, he then shears two sheep – the first the old way with hand shears, and the second at speed with electric clippers.

Despite a few ups and downs, it has been a very successful little business, particularly as the cruise ships which call at Napier have put the show on their list of land-based activities. As Angus observes: 'We were lucky, because the cruise ships put it on their activity list. In the season, we do up to about 20 boats with about 100 people at a time.'

In 2003, Angus decided he'd had enough of the day-to-day running of Clifton, and that he wanted to write the history of the Gordon family at Clifton. So he leased out the backcountry

(665.5 hectares) to Graham Lowe, who had bought neighbouring Taurapa some years before, and set out to write a comprehensive history of the station. He enjoyed the process of researching and writing very much, and two years later the finished product was published as *In the Shadow of the Cape: A History of the Gordon Family at Clifton*.

He had retained the flats, and once again successfully grew squash mixed with some maize and wheat.

MISHAPS

Until Angus came along, serious accidents on the farm were rare. But single-handedly he managed to increase the number by about 100-fold. The first serious one happened in 1971, when he and John Orsborn were cutting up large gum-tree branches that had fallen across the road. Angus's chainsaw hit a piece of wire imbedded in the tree and bounced back into his face. He recalls: 'All I felt was a thump, but no pain. The chainsaw had hit my left jaw, opening it right up and smashing a tooth at the same time. It just missed the jugular vein by a hair's breadth, before finishing off in the fleshy part of my chest below the shoulder.'

John rushed him to hospital where he was stitched up: 'Forty stitches were used all around my mouth, jaw and shoulder. When John Orsborn came to see me the next day, he was surprised. He was sure that I would be deformed for life when he saw the whole of my left jaw opened up!'

In 1992, Angus had another near-miss when his four-wheeler farm bike tipped up and rolled

OPPOSITE
Angus mustering in his Can-Am.

on him, right out at the back of the farm. It threw the dogs clear but hurled him right into the path of the overturning machine, which flipped over and came down on top of him. Despite extensive injuries, somehow he managed to right the bike. He made it to the road, where he was picked up by a neighbour and taken to Clifton. Dinah rushed him to hospital where a haemorrhaging punctured lung, a broken collarbone and 12 broken ribs were diagnosed. After two weeks in hospital, he went home to a slow and tedious convalescence.

In 2013, he got stomped on by a cow, which broke his shoulder socket and dislocated both shoulders. Another trip ensued, this time in the helicopter, to Napier hospital. It is no wonder that Dinah has said: 'When Angus disappears I worry now! He went off to look at Charles's hill one day and rang me at 5 o'clock in the evening to say he had slid sideways on the ute, which was now lying on its side in the dam! Would I come and get him . . . I had no idea what I was going to find. I rushed along hoping he wasn't still under water.'

Luckily he had managed to get out of the ute, and for once had done himself no damage, so Dinah took him home on the motorbike.

A NEW GENERATION

As it did with his own parents, the issue of succession continues to occupy Angus's mind. He explains: 'Inheritance is a huge issue with landowners today. Many families have had to sell their farms. What I have farmed for all my life is to be able to hand Clifton over as I got it or in an even better position.'

Because the farm is small and difficult to farm, dividing it between Tom and his sister, Abby, is not an option, so it will go in its entirety to Tom. And like John and Barbara, Angus and Dinah have been very concerned to make provision for their daughter. So they have bought or developed other assets – such as the Vanuatu property and the café. But it is, perhaps, not as easy to equalise inheritance today as it was in John and Barbara's time, because of the huge rise in the value of coastal properties. As Angus points out, when he inherited Clifton, 'it had nowhere near the value it has today. In fact the Old Man believed it was a bit of a liability.'

Today, beautiful accessible coastal properties such as Clifton,

OPPOSITE TOP
Tallying up.

OPPOSITE BOTTOM
Mustering.

within easy reach of the towns, have become hugely sought-after, with large sums of money paid to acquire them.

FATHER-AND-SON PARTNERSHIP

Angus and Dinah's son, Tom, who had been away at university and overseas, returned to Clifton in 2007 keen to start farming. Like his father, Tom has a great love for Clifton: 'I always wanted to be a farmer and I always wanted to live here. I love being on the farm. I love just running around out on the hills. It's a pretty cool farm; there are wild goats, turkeys, the river and the rapids – so much stuff to see and do. I used to love going up the river and playing in the hay barn with (cousins) Rupert, Isabel and Lily, and all those kinds of things. So that's just the natural progression that you start running it one day.'

However, with the land leased out, there was only summer work for him, helping with the cropping. After a summer of farm work, Tom decided to go to Japan for the winter to do farm shows there for a New Zealand company. At the same time he started his own small

ABOVE
After university, Abby trained as a pilot and found work flying small planes in West Papua. She worked there for three years, flying in difficult conditions to inaccessible villages, with nothing more than a paddock to land on. In mid-2015 she and her Norwegian partner, Michael, also a pilot, moved to Norway, where she is retraining to be able to fly there. GORDON FAMILY COLLECTION

OPPOSITE
Tom on his bike.

enterprise at Clifton: 'With the money I had made in Japan, I tried to start a little hay-making business. I planted about 8 hectares of lucerne and bought a tractor, a hay-baler and a hay-mower, and did a couple of seasons. Then, unfortunately, the lucerne all got buried beneath a couple of feet of silt in the 2011 flood, so I lost all that crop. We have slowly been fixing all that land down there and this year (2015) I have got lucerne back there again.'

After four years of travelling back and forth to Japan, he and Angus decided to take the farm back at the end of 2011, just as a 'weather bomb' devastated the farm. As had happened in 1974, the fences were nearly all taken out by slips, stock was lost, and it was generally a terrible mess.

Angus recalls: 'Although it was a bad time in a way, because the farm was in such a mess, Tom and I decided to go into partnership and started a company called Gordon Farming Limited. We took over the farm at the beginning of 2012. At this stage, because we had no stock of our own, we decided to change the policy from being a breeding sheep and wool place to being a lamb-fattening place.'

They could only fatten lambs in winter, so they bought 200 cows,

ABOVE
Sheep on the side of the hill.

OPPOSITE TOP
Sheep in the new woolshed yards.

OPPOSITE BOTTOM
Tom mustering for the sheep show.

grazers, Wagyus and others to help keep the country clean in summer. This system has now been in place for three years and is working well, with the lambs leaving the property in the first week of November when everything begins to dry out. 'We fatten 4000 to 5000 lambs over winter for a company called CR Grace Limited; we just fatten them on a weight-gains basis.'

Once the lambs leave, 'the country is left for the cows to clean up over the summer. We have no sheep on, so that in the massive drought the year after we took over, we had plenty of grass. In fact we took on grazers that year, we had so much residual grass left over from spring. We have a very, very simple policy!'

Tom adds: 'Clifton is a hard-work farm, big paddocks, steep, dry, probably not great pastures compared to a lot of other farms, so we just have to farm to our strengths, which is that it is early. It doesn't get frosts so we start growing grass earlier in the spring, which means we can fatten lambs.'

> 'It is the most delightful thing I have done . . . I just love working with my son every day. He and I get on well.'

The father–son equal partnership has been a great success. Angus believes that: 'It is the most delightful thing I have done. When I gave up farming in 2002, I had had enough of it. It was

OPPOSITE
Taking a tea break.

hard yakka and we were going nowhere, the prices were always bad, it seemed to be nothing but down, down. Since I have taken over with Tom, we don't seem to make much more money out of the farm, but I just love working with my son every day. He and I get on well.'

Tom agrees: 'I love working with Dad, he is pretty easy-going. Whenever we've got a rainy day or a spare moment, we sit around planning things and working out what we want to do, how we are going to do it. We are always trying to figure out new schemes, come up with new ideas, bouncing them off each other.'

Like his father before him, Tom is always looking for new ways to optimise land use and make the best living possible off the land, which is why he decided to lease 20 hectares of the flat land to Ben Bostock for five years, who is going to turn it organic to grow grain for his chickens. Another 7 hectares are being leased out to a nectarine grower. Developing tourist accommodation is another idea that both Tom and his wife, Lucia, are keen on. They have already invested in a special tent for 'upmarket glamping' out on the farm. And Tom is once again growing lucerne on the flats, so he can fatten lambs over the summer months.

Despite the difficulties of farming such a steep, dry farm, six generations have loved living on the property and aim to continue doing so. As Lucia points out: 'It is beautiful living here . . . it has got everything, everything you could ever want, going

FOLLOWING SPREAD
Glamping overlooking the river.

OPPOSITE
Tom going fishing with Brian Chalmers after a day's work on the farm, watched by Lucia and Frankie.

out on the farm on the bike, the sea and all at our back doorstep. Every time you come home and you drive round that corner you think, "Oh wow!" But also you are not isolated, the village is just down the road, Hastings is about 20 minutes away, a quarter-hour from Havelock, my parents live down the road, there's a shop nearby, there's wineries, everything we could ever need.'

'That's the whole point of living here really; it's not about the farming so much, the farming is what you do to be able to live – it's about the joy of living here.'

Tom adds, 'That's the whole point of living here really; it's not about the farming so much, the farming is what you do to be able to live – it's about the joy of living here.'

TOM AND LUCIA

Tom and Lucia have known each other pretty much all of their lives – their parents having been friends meant that they played together as children. One of four girls, Lucia grew up in Havelock North. After years of travelling, working as a chef on the super-yachts in Europe and living in Vanuatu, amongst other places, she returned to Auckland to work as a chef. While living in Auckland, she reconnected with Tom, and eventually moved back to Hawke's Bay so that they could be together. Their daughter, Francesca Nicola Gordon, known as Frankie, was born 26 June 2015, making her the seventh generation of Gordons to live at Clifton. Lucia and Tom got married in March 2016.

OPPOSITE
Tom and his daughter, Francesca (Frankie).

CHAPTER SEVEN

SUMMERLEE/ CAPE KIDNAPPERS
A Remarkable Transformation

Summerlee Station, which had been cut off from Clifton and sold to the Neilson family in 1926, evolved in unexpected ways from the late 1990s onwards. Formerly a sheep farm occupying some magnificent but challenging terrain, it acquired new owners, new assets, and a variety of surprising new roles. In the early years of the twenty-first century, the Cape Kidnappers' landscape remains spectacular and unspoiled. Sheep and cattle still graze there. But it is now a 'multiple-use landscape', home also to award-winning tourism and ecotourism facilities, forestry, and a ground-breaking nature sanctuary renowned for its conservation programmes.

The first stage in this remarkable transformation commenced in 1996, when Andrew and Michael Neilson sold Summerlee to Wellingtonians Charlotte and Robert Fisher. Robert already had an interest in the station, having bought the stock several years previously, and farmed it for a time in partnership with the Neilson brothers. Upon becoming sole owner, he started an extensive upgrade. This, he recalls, incorporated: 'all facets of the sheep station, homestead and ground. It included animal husbandry, a large increase in stock numbers, from under 2500 stock up to 9000, installation and repair of 12 dams, a fertiliser programme, renewal of pasture, a major fencing programme – approximately 9 kilometres – a total plant and machinery upgrade, 9-kilometre metal farm roading out to the Cape, plus renewal of several kilometres of farm-bike tracks, the trapping and night-shooting of approximately 3500 possums, and eradication of approximately 900 feral goats.'

Fisher also fenced off about 180 hectares of bush known as the Rough Block, as a conservation area, where, as part of an ongoing

Hawke's Bay wide programme, the regional council instigated a possum-control programme. 'We were amazed at the size of this native block and the plethora of different native species. Once we had done the eradication programme of possums and fenced it off from stock, the block regenerated in a very short time.'

The 1926 homestead on Karaka Hill required renovating from the roof down. 'The scale of the renovation,' Fisher recalls, 'was such that to justify the exercise, we decided to operate it commercially as a luxury retreat. We therefore put in a tennis court, swimming pool and created a 10-acre garden and grounds by eradicating the area of box hawthorn and wild blackberry.'

The Fishers built themselves a smaller house further down the hill and ran Summerlee House for many years as a luxury lodge. They sold Summerlee House in April 2015 to an Auckland family, but still own the smaller house.

Upon purchasing Summerlee, Fisher also took over a small enterprise the Neilsons were running, driving tourists overland to

BELOW
Summerlee House.

the gannet colony. Gannet Safaris Overland has subsequently grown exponentially. Having started with one small vehicle, it now boasts a fleet of six buses, two mini-vans and a Range Rover. Many customers come from the cruise ships that visit Napier during the season. Robert's sister, Jo Fisher, a driver/tour guide for the company since 2000, has noticed that gannet-tour customers 'have steadily increased, particularly with the arrival of cruise ships. When I first came here, there were one or perhaps two vans. Just individuals and small groups of private people, and then the cruise ships started coming in and that really upped the business.' Gannet-tour visitor numbers are currently about 8000 annually and still increasing.

    Not all visitors are from overseas. 'At first we didn't get many New Zealanders, as most people went along the beach on the trailers; it was a cheaper option for getting there. But now, local tourism to Hawke's Bay has increased, and more and more New Zealanders are coming with us because they have heard how lovely our trip is. Now about a third are New Zealanders. Lots of people just come off

the road, and just get on a bus and we drive them out there slowly, giving a running commentary all the way. It is a terribly interesting, traditional New Zealand farm, and of course a lot of people don't have the opportunity to get onto a traditional farm these days. Quite often we are in a mob of sheep or cattle en route, and you can often see them mustering from the distance, and there are sheep in the yards and so on.'

For Jo, getting to the colony is a key part of the experience: 'You drive through this beautiful property up above the sea . . . we drive along the tops of the cliffs literally, and stop on the top so people can get photos, you are 600 feet up and time and again people say to me that the trip is better than the actual gannets!'

In 2002, the Fishers sold the farm to Americans, Julian and Josie Robertson, but kept Summerlee House and some cottages. Julian Robertson, who already owned Kauri Cliffs Golf Course in Northland, had been looking for a second golf course and lodge destination that would show international golfers another aspect of New Zealand. Summerlee fitted the bill.

> 'You drive through this beautiful property up above the sea . . . You are 600 feet up and time and again people say to me that the trip is better than the actual gannets!'

The Robertsons first visited New Zealand for about six months in 1978. As Julian remembers: 'I am a geographer – I've always loved geography, and I'd heard that New Zealand had the most complex geography of any place in the English-speaking world. So I came out with my wife and children, aged four and one, and found that turned out to be true.'

Nearly 20 years later, a friend, keen to find a bolthole in New Zealand far from the United States and its problems, asked Robertson if he, too, might be interested in finding a property there: 'A friend, very worried about the race riots in Watts [Los Angeles], planned to get some property in New Zealand. He rang me and said: "You lived there

OPPOSITE TOP
View on the way to the gannet colony.

OPPOSITE BOTTOM
Gannet Safaris at the gannet colony.

A Gift of Gannets: The World's Most Accessible Mainland Colony

On 27 January 1910, Wellington's *Dominion* newspaper reported:

> Wanton cruelty is reported in reference to the young gannets around Cape Kidnappers by certain thoughtless and callous persons. The offenders are said to have taken the young birds from their nests and thrown them over the precipice, to see if they could fly. In consequence of this they were dashed to pieces at the bottom of the cliff.

The article concluded with the observation that the gannet colony was 'really a scenic asset to Hawke's Bay, and one that should be conserved in every way possible'. Frank Gordon agreed wholeheartedly with this sentiment, and in January 1915, fed up with vandals repeatedly harming the gannet colony at Cape Kidnappers, he took action. While in

ABOVE
Beach safaris to the gannets.

OPPOSITE
Gannets with the lighthouse in the background.

Wellington as chairman of the county council, he visited Minister of Lands WJ Massey and made a proposal. For the safety of the birds, and for the public's enjoyment, he offered the 32 acres (13 hectares) that comprised Cape Kidnappers to the government on the understanding that it become a gannet reserve in perpetuity. The minister gratefully accepted, later writing to thank Frank for this 'public-spirited action'. Frank became one of the founding members of a special board set up to manage the reserve. This board appointed honorary wardens who helped to protect the birds whenever they could.

There are currently over 20,000 birds at four major nesting sites: the Plateau, Saddle, Whalebone Reef and Black Reef. The large elegant birds, with gold-tipped crowns and black-tipped feathers, mate for life, and breed at the Cape between August and April. To feed, they dive-bomb straight out of the sky into the sea, wings at first half-open and then, at the moment of impact, closed. They can spot fish from great heights. Sometimes whole flocks plummet into the sea at speeds of up to 145 kilometres per hour. Visiting the colony is now one of the most popular tourist attractions in Hawke's Bay. Two businesses, Gannet Beach Adventures and Gannet Safaris, offer tours along the spectacular coast from Clifton to Kidnappers to view the colony. A percentage of the fees for this adventure goes to the Department of Conservation. The gannet reserve is closed between 1 July and the Wednesday before Labour Weekend, to protect breeding pairs.

for a while, would you like for me to look at some property for you?" He said he had a representative over there who would be glad to look for me. So I told him that if he could find something in Northland I would be interested. And he came up with Kauri Cliffs. It is gorgeous.'

When Robertson later heard that Cape Kidnappers might be for sale, he couldn't resist the opportunity, because: 'It was so very beautiful and I had such good luck with Kauri Cliffs: I just couldn't turn down Cape Kidnappers as a golf course.'

Before long he had 'made an offer on an extremely beautiful coastline property in the North Island that cost not much more than the price of a modest New York apartment.'

Where Kauri Cliffs is gentle, lush, green country, Summerlee is rugged and uncompromising, with long, dry summer droughts. For Robertson, 'These courses reflect the natural beauty of this magnificent country, and are microcosms of their surrounding area.'

He immediately commenced turning the plateau land above the cliffs into a spectacular golf course. 'Actually turning it into a golf

BELOW
The Cape, looking back over Cape Kidnappers farm.

course wasn't difficult, as the course is reasonably flat except for a few holes . . . but [building] the road was the biggest shock I have ever had. I bought the land and I was thrilled about it, and then somebody said you will have to put a road in – that was a surprise – it was a major!'

He had to build an all-weather sealed two-lane 7-kilometre road with 13 bridges in place of an old dirt access track that had followed the river-bed and was often impassable in winter.

Noted golf course architect Tom Doak then designed the Cape Kidnappers course, situated on top of a series of ridges that jut out to cliffs, which drop vertically to the sea about 160 metres below. The valleys or ravines between the ridges, left in native trees and bush, are linked by long, narrow bridges for the golfers to get across. Michael Hiller, writing in *Avid Golfer*, paid tribute to Doak's skill: '[he] stitched together jagged fingers of land in a dramatic series of fairways, routing them out and back like they were fingers of a glove. Errant shots left or right almost certainly fall into the ocean or an abyss . . . most golfers reach for their cameras.'

New Zealand Golf Blog noted in 2008 that '. . . the site is not like anywhere else in golf. It is an overwhelming experience to stand up on the cliffs, 140 metres above sea level and look out across the waves far below in Hawke's Bay.'

Jonathan McCord, the resident head professional at Kidnappers, comments: 'To have a golf course on such a spectacular piece of land, perched 167 metres above sea level, it's quite unique . . . it's stunning. People often take more time taking pictures than playing golf!'

Since opening, Cape Kidnappers has been consistently voted one of the top 50 golf courses in the world. A five-star luxury lodge, known as The Farm at Cape Kidnappers, opened in November 2007, but not after a certain amount of controversy.

> **'To have a golf course on such a spectacular piece of land, perched 167 metres above sea level, it's quite unique . . . it's stunning. People often take more time taking pictures than playing golf!'**

In December 2003, Hastings District Council, despite having designated the area an Outstanding Natural Feature 5 – an ONF5 prohibits any development that would compromise the visual integrity of the natural features – granted resource consent for a lodge much further out on the Black Reef headland. To build this facility, perched on the cliffs above the ocean overlooking the sea and beach below, would have entailed tunnelling a room into a western cliff face 'to provide sunset views'. In October 2004, three locals, Rod Heaps, owner of Gannet Beach Adventures, Peter Nee Harland, a member of a local hapū, and Charles Gordon, John and Barbara Gordon's youngest son, appealed to the Environment Court to get the council's consent overturned, citing 'the adverse effects such a lodge may have on the landscape and amenities of its surrounding environment'.

Two months later, in December of that year, the court overturned the Hastings District Council's resource consent on the grounds that the Cape was a unique and iconic landscape. As the judges concluded: 'It

OPPOSITE TOP
Looking back towards the cliffs of Clifton beach from the golf course.

OPPOSITE BOTTOM
Golf course on fingers of land jutting into the sea.

seems to us to be beyond argument that the introduction of that level of activity into this site will have adverse effects on the environment . . . and the area covered by the ONF overlay is a unique, iconic landscape with intense amenity values. It takes very little that is man-made to jar there . . .' As a result the lodge was re-sited.

The lodge at Cape Kidnappers, named The Farm, opened its doors to visitors in November 2007. Guests to the lodge, drawn from all over the world, enjoy the sweeping views, play golf, visit the gannets, walk the scenic tracks, and go on farm tours.

The station still remains a working sheep and cattle farm. Manager Alex Tuanui runs some 5500 stock units on the block, and there are also 400 hectares of forest. Since 2009, lodge visitors have also enjoyed Kiwi Discovery Walks. This latter attraction allows them to assist in one of the many projects undertaken by the Cape Kidnappers Sanctuary. The lodge, golf course and gannet colony are all situated within this now internationally renowned enclave that traverses three privately-owned properties on the Cape.

PREVIOUS SPREAD
Road to the golf course.

ABOVE
Aerial view of the lodge.

OPPOSITE
Lodge entrance.

Julian Robertson

Julian Robertson, a native of North Carolina and now-retired hedge-fund manager, has long been one of this country's most enthusiastic admirers. Interviewed in the *Dominion Post* in 2010, he observed: 'I think New Zealand was put on this earth as the greatest tourist destination there is.' Pointing towards the Cape Kidnappers fairways he added: 'You can't find anything like that golf course anywhere else . . . It's the most gorgeous land in the world.'

In addition to establishing and investing in

ABOVE
Julian holding a kiwi.

various business enterprises in New Zealand, Robertson has, over the years, earned gratitude and respect for his generous, ongoing philanthropy. In 2009, he and his wife, Josie, donated an art collection worth $115 million to Auckland Art Gallery. Robertson gave $5 million to the Christchurch earthquake relief fund in 2011, and in 2012 donated $5.3 million dollars to found the New Zealand Antarctic Research Institute.

The Robertson Foundation, set up in 1996, has over $1 billion in assets and offers high-impact grants in the United States. Sir John Hood, a former vice chancellor of the University of Auckland and of Oxford University, currently heads this foundation. The Aotearoa Foundation, an affiliate foundation, makes grants within New Zealand, focusing in three main areas: education, the environment, and medical research.

In December 2009, Julian Robertson was made an Honorary Knight Companion of the New Zealand Order of Merit for services to business and philanthropy. The 2011 investiture ceremony at the New Zealand Embassy in Washington was in many ways also a tribute to Josie Robertson, who died in June 2010 after a long battle with breast cancer. She had been her husband's partner in philanthropy and shared his love of New Zealand. Julian Robertson later described the investiture and black-tie dinner as 'a great night, just done perfectly . . . It was a very emotional experience for me because New Zealand was a real love affair between my wife and me and the country . . . I can't tell you the number of times she'd wake up in the morning and look outside and say, "We're in paradise."'

CHAPTER EIGHT
THE HANSENS OF HAUPOURI

Haupouri had been carved off Clifton in 1907 for Edward Gordon, who following his death in 1914, left it in three equal shares to his nephews Lindsay, Mick and Ian. Mick and Ian bought out Lindsay's share and jointly owned both Taurapa and Haupouri. When Ian married in 1933, ownership of the two properties separated, with Mick taking Taurapa and Ian getting Haupouri. After Ian died in 1983, Paul Robinson managed the farm until Ian's granddaughter, Juliet, and her husband, Warwick Hansen, took it over in 1988.

At that stage the farm was a regular beef and sheep station. Because that kind of farming was getting progressively more difficult, the couple soon started looking at other options. Warwick, formerly a top New Zealand show-jumper, decided to build a horse-breeding facility. In 1995, with former All Black David Kirk as partner, he founded New Zealand Performance Horses (NZPH), and started breeding horses using imported frozen semen from France. He recalls: 'I got to nearly the end of my time show-jumping and the sport was saying we have the riders in New Zealand but we don't have the horse power. So I decided to go to France in 1992 to look for the best horses we could breed from and from which we could bring in frozen semen. So I brought that in and we started to breed our own mares.'

That was 20 years ago. Today, there are about 150 horses on the property, at least 30 of them brood mares, with many more having been successfully sold over the years. NZPH has become the biggest sport horse-breeder in Australasia, and their horses are sold in both Australasia and further afield. Horses they have bred and trained participate in show-jumping and eventing in Japan, America and

PREVIOUS SPREAD
Horses on Haupouri Hills.

OPPOSITE
Haupouri woolshed on Ocean Beach.

England. As Warwick notes: 'You can't go to a show in Australia without seeing an NZPH horse.'

Juliet and Warwick's younger daughter, Bridget, who was born in 1993, has followed in her father's footsteps and has become one of New Zealand's top young riders. She is now the face of NZPH in Australia, where she spends a large part of the year. Warwick explains 'When she was 17, she wanted to compete in Australia, so I put her on a plane with five horses and she went to Australia for the winter. Now she spends six months here and six months in Australia. She takes some of our best horses, the ones that will suit the Australian market – and sells them over there.'

At the same time, Warwick and Juliet still run a beef and sheep operation, which, despite the success of the horses, remains their biggest earner. As farming became more difficult and they had to lay off staff, Juliet found herself much more involved in running the sheep and cattle. 'Birdie [Bridget] went to school at five and farming was really getting tough, so, with the exception of one general hand, we got rid of our boys and men so that we had nobody on Haupouri. I got a team of dogs and went full-time. It was just me and Warwick, just the two of us did all of the Haupouri stock work. They were big paddocks and it was hard work then.'

It was a long, hard day. Not only was Juliet shepherding full-time, she had to drive to Havelock North twice a day for the girls' schooling, and keep the house running without any extra help. 'I carried on shepherding for about eight to 10 years, then had a stint of not doing so much farm work, but now I have gone back and I work seven days a week now. Now in winter I do the bulls, seven days, twice a day, shifting them or feeding them morning and night. It is quite full on . . . I do all sorts of other general maintenance jobs. I have gone from being full-time shepherd to handyman. I will do everything . . . I just fill in whenever they need somebody.'

In the past few years, the cattle-farming side has changed from breeding cows to fattening bulls. 'We have between 1000 and 1500 bulls . . . We buy them in at 18 months and sell them at two to two-and-a-half. We buy them in March and sell most of them at Christmas time.'

Recently the Hansens' eldest daughter, Hillary, who returned to the farm in 2011 after gaining a Bachelor of Business Studies from

OPPOSITE
Juliet and Warwick Hansen.

AUT, has taken over this operation. Hillary is keen to introduce more technology into this process, with specialised feeding and a regular weighing programme. She has also transformed the sheep operation into specially developing lambs for Coastal Spring Lamb, a Whanganui-based company specialising in early lamb delivered direct to local supermarkets. Warwick explains: 'We used to have 7000 ewes, but now we are down to 4000 ewes for early lambs and these lambs are hopefully gone by the end of January. The lambs are born in early July . . . ours are going to Havelock and Hastings New Worlds, starting in October.'

Farming has become much simpler for the Hansens in recent years. 'The real idea of our farming is that we know we are going to struggle between the months of January to March with no grass and droughts, so no bulls on and no lambs on, all we are doing are ewes. Very simple . . . So it has taken the hassle of huge droughts away from us, which was our biggest issue. Organised, productive farming to minimise risk where possible is our future outlook.'

Farming Haupouri has been very tough, with endless droughts, bad markets, and then the 2011 weather bomb, which almost wiped them out completely. After 800 millilitres of rain fell in just 48 hours, the saturated hills started slipping, taking out fences, covering pastures with silt, and destroying all the roads and tracks. It was the worst rain ever recorded in the area. 'We have records that go back 140 years and that was definitely the worst ever – it was a one in 500 year storm for us.'

They reckon they lost about 40 per cent of their land, which was

BELOW
Haupouri stables.

a crippling blow. 'It was all so crazy', Warwick observes, 'We battled droughts for four years and made it through, and in two days it was all gone.'

The repair cost was enormous. Thirty-five kilometres of roads had to be rebuilt, and nearly every paddock refenced.

Since their arrival at the farm in 1988, Juliet and Warwick had been trying to find ways to buy out her two brothers' share of the farm. Farming alone wasn't going to provide enough funds, so they tried to subdivide some land off for houses. That was just getting underway when Julian Robertson bought neighbouring Summerlee Station and the value of Haupouri skyrocketed. They faced either selling the whole farm – which for the family was 'not an option' or selling part of it. Consequently, in late 2002, they went into partnership with Andy Lowe – who owns neighbouring Taurapa – on the 578-hectare coastal strip and sold him another 28 hectares outright, including the land around the woolshed. They plan to build a new woolshed, utility sheds, yards and so on, further up on top, 'away from the beach and potential problems of tsunamis, fires, tourists and so forth'.

At the same time they will build themselves a new house nearby, because as part of a rationalisation and consolidation process they have sold the main homestead to their business partner, David Kirk.

Despite the hardships and knockbacks, the Hansens are determined to stay at Haupouri: 'The ultimate dream was to retain as much of Haupouri as we can. We are not here to make money. We love this place and we have two younger family members who want to be here and farm the land forever. We're here to stay.'

CHAPTER NINE

CREATING THE CAPE SANCTUARY

In 2002, local businessman Andy Lowe bought a portion of Haupouri Station. This land, which shares a 6-kilometre boundary with Summerlee, features 290 hectares of sand dunes and about 11 kilometres of beach. Before purchasing the property, Lowe, a keen outdoorsman with a strong interest in New Zealand fauna and flora, realised the special ecological and historical nature of the area.

He recalls how he first became convinced of the need to conserve it: 'It all came about through looking at the beach when I went down there. I read some reports that had been done by an ecologist, who talked about how, from an ecological point of view, it was pretty special because of the sand dunes, which in Hawke's Bay are now very rare. Most of Hawke's Bay's dune systems have been grazed, wrecked, erased or have plant life on them . . . The excavations showed that a very wide variety of native fauna had originally been there – tuatara, moa, pāteke, takahē, raven, and so on. It was also an important spiritual place for Māori, with the Cape being the hook of Māui . . . There were Māori bones and pā sites, and there are all the pā sites on the hills, and you have Colenso's track going through there, so you have the European history as well. You look at this place and think: we have got to save all this.'

There was also the unique Rough Block on Summerlee, the 180-hectare patch of native forest that Robert Fisher had fenced off in 1996 and which, Lowe appreciated, was 'the only coastal forest around for miles . . . It was the last coastal remnant of what used to be.' This land had survived intact because it was too steep and infertile for farming. Despite fire, some grazing, and the introduction of weeds, an array of palatable plants somehow managed to survive

OPPOSITE
Present-day map showing the Clifton, Tauraroa, Haupouri and Cape Kidnappers stations.
SURVEYING THE BAY

in its deep gorges, on ledges and rock walls beyond the reach of goats and possums. Pest control in the Rough Block had also been underway for some years, to great effect. Feral pigs had long been completely exterminated, and possums were almost extinct; in 2002 and 2003 contractors shot more than 3000 of them. In the late 1990s, for example, hunters shot more than 2000 feral goats on the Cape Kidnappers headland in a single week. By 2009, they, too, had been eliminated after concerted eradication campaigns.

Apart from the forest in the Rough Block, however, the land on Cape Kidnappers peninsula, like most coastal farms throughout New Zealand, was more or less completely denuded of native flora and fauna. The gannet colony at the tip of the peninsula was one notable exception, and there were also some small forest birds such as fantails, grey warblers, silvereyes and bellbirds in patches of woody vegetation. Andy recognised the area's conservation potential, but wondered how to achieve it. Eventually he hit upon the solution: a sanctuary that would help to re-establish native species and foster and protect regionally rare reptiles, birds and native plants.

From the outset Andy realised that other activities in the area, such as farming, tourism, forestry and recreation, needed to be accommodated. In his view: 'You have to do it differently. You have got to do it in a sustainable way, where farming can coexist with recreation, and then you have all the recreational people who want to use this place, and then you have the people who actually live here. So the project started as a sort of new-age way of doing conservation, where human recreation and farming and forestry could cohabit with endangered species.'

Andy's desire to create a sanctuary was so strong that he made sure it was stipulated in the sale and purchase agreement of Haupouri: 'Before I bought into Haupouri I had done enough research to know this stuff had to be saved . . . it was in the original sale and purchase agreement that I had the right to do it . . . that I could put a vermin-proof fence on it if I could get Julian Robertson to agree.'

Robertson was very happy to proceed with the fence; so, too, were the Hansen family, who still owned 890 hectares of Haupouri, and were partners with the Lowe family in the 578-hectare coastal strip.

As a result of his growing sense that the Ocean Beach area was particularly special from a historical and archaeological perspective,

ABOVE
Tuatara

and that sustainable conservation required human interaction, Andy, under the auspices of his property development company Hill Country Corporation, wanted to build a housing development at the southern end of the beach and covenant the rest of the beach for conservation. Quoted in *Hawke's Bay Today* in October 2006, he explained: 'What I am having a crack at doing is having all land owners [there are six] work together for a hundred-year plan so we don't get a hodgepodge of development down the coast – people just using their rights.'

His vision was 'a multicultural European type sustainable village for all walks of society, a seaside village for Hawke's Bay on a finite area – about ten per cent of the beach so that the rest of it could be protected'. He wanted a village that the average Kiwi could afford: 'Average Kiwis want to be able to live and enjoy the beach and you have two options – you either have a few big sections which are worth over a million dollars each, or you create a community where different sections of the community can participate.'

To solicit responses to the proposals, a consultation process or 'charrette' commenced, jointly funded by Hastings District Council and Andy Lowe's Hill Country Corporation. From 5 October 2005, members of the public could take part and express their views in a 10-day planning and design workshop, held in Haupouri woolshed, and facilitated by American firm DPZ Pacific, and Australian urban designers and town planners, Roberts Day. The purpose of this charrette, according to a *Dominion Post* interview with Hastings mayor Lawrence Yule, was to enable 'all parties to put their dreams and concerns on the table before going through the more cumbersome and legal Resource Management Act process. It was a non-binding hui that covered all issues, from the style of architecture to plant life on the beach.'

The *Dominion Post*, reporting on the proposed development plans on 8 April 2006, described a village of 980 dwellings, including a main street, plaza and buildings up to four storeys high with ground-floor shops and offices. The main village could also house 200 apartments. 'The plans also include a primary school, hotel and church. A smaller village to the south – on what is now Māori owned land – is earmarked for 224 dwellings and an 81-dwelling hamlet is also planned.'

The public response to the proposal grew increasingly loud and negative, culminating in an 8000-signature petition in February 2008 against allowing the development to proceed. Bending to public opinion, the council voted to oppose it, commissioned an independent study of possible plans, and in September presented its own plan-change options. In October 2008, Hill Country Corporation withdrew its application for a private plan change for the beach. As Andy explained: 'In the end it just got too hard, some Māori were happy to go along with it and some weren't, and it just got too political, so I just pulled out.'

As part of the Hastings District Council's review of its district plan in 2015, the council has proposed a new and unique nature preservation zone across Ocean Beach and Cape Kidnappers. This would limit residential and commercial activity to specific small areas, provided it has a conservation purpose or is required to support conservation activities. This proposal, however, is being challenged in the Environmental Court.

SANCTUARY BEGINNINGS

Andy Lowe approached the distinguished ecologist John McLennan – who had spent most of his career studying kiwi and what could be done to save them – and presented his idea for the sanctuary. McLennan recalls: 'I was hugely excited by it because it pushed me into a direction that I wanted to see conservation unfolding in New Zealand . . . Worldwide biodiversity is declining at quite an alarming rate. We all know that, and it is just a tired old message, but the reality is that we actually *need* to save biodiversity . . . But across the world, spaces that can be used exclusively for sanctuaries and biodiversity conservation are becoming rarer and rarer. So we have to work with what we've got. We have to save species and ecosystems in the presence of people. We have got to do it where people live, work and play, and that to my knowledge had never been attempted in New Zealand. Historically we have had a clear distinction between what is conservation and what is production land, we have always had such a low population density. But that can't go on forever, and Andy was the first to suggest a sanctuary that blurred the lines. I wanted to help Andy show New Zealand that sanctuaries in these sort of production landscapes can produce outstanding biodiversity results. So I jumped on board.'

In 2005, McLennan presented a report to the landowners recommending the first conservation steps required, and the species to be introduced. Once the landowners accepted this plan, work started on pest control and research commenced into the best type of fence to keep pests out.

Tamsin Ward-Smith, who had previously worked for the Department of Conservation, started managing the Cape Sanctuary in 2006. It was a formative time, as 'nothing was then underway, the idea had just started'.

Pest control began immediately, even before the fence went in, and took the form of intensive trapping, poisoning and shooting. Ward-Smith focused mainly on stoats, rats, ferrets and wild cats, because possums and goats were already at low levels thanks to previous control efforts by Hawke's Bay Regional Council and local farmers. Two capable colleagues assisted her: 'Lance Drew and then Travis Cullen [who managed pest control at the sanctuary for seven years until 2014] helped me set it up. We built and installed about

1200 trap boxes for stoats, weasels and ferrets, and then we started installing the bait stations. We are now up to 2500 stations for rats. They are on a very tight grid.'

At the end of 2006, after trialling various fence systems and meshes, the fence finally started being built. Upon completion in December 2007, it extended about 10.6 kilometres across the base of Cape Kidnappers peninsula from coast to coast, although as Andy Lowe points out: 'If you measured it by going up and down the valleys and hills, it would be more like 15 kilometres.' It encloses about 2500 hectares of land, and is thus larger than many wildlife refuges on offshore islands. Unusually, it is a 'leaky system', meaning that the ends on the coast are open, and can be up to 30 metres wide at low tide, allowing the pests to trickle back into the sanctuary. However, the fence significantly reduces re-invasion rates, and when combined with the intensive pest-eradication programme, has resulted in 'near zero pest densities' for most of the time.

An additional fence built inside the sanctuary after 2007 provides a predator-free environment for various reptiles, invertebrates and nesting petrels. It is 610 metres long and encloses 2 hectares of steep terrain on a headland at the north end of Ocean Beach. With the exception of three mice incursions, which were quickly dealt with, this

ABOVE
A drop of poisoned carrots to get rid of the rabbits within the sanctuary.
CAPE SANCTUARY COLLECTION

space has been almost entirely pest-free. Another fence, 4000 metres long and 1.2 metres high, built to prevent various flightless birds (takahē initially) from dispersing throughout the wider sanctuary, encloses 90 hectares of coastal faces immediately behind the Ocean Beach dunes.

DUNE RESTORATION: TREASURES WORTH PRESERVING

Coastal dune systems are one of New Zealand's most endangered environments. The 290 hectares of dunes at Ocean Beach contain significant fossil and archaeological sites, and numerous species of increasingly rare animals and plants. In addition to being visually spectacular, these dune systems are among the least modified in the country, which makes their protection a priority. In 2008, the area was fenced off and, aided by a sizeable grant from the Government Biodiversity Condition Fund, a weed control programme was initiated.

To re-establish native plants on the dunes and surrounding hinterland, an intensive planting programme commenced. Hundreds of volunteers spent weeks planting native sand tussock, coastal shrub daisy seedlings, and sand and shore milkweed along with various shrubs and trees to 'recreate the low windswept forest that used to grow there several hundred years ago'.

The Lowe family have planted 250,000 native trees on the slopes behind the dunes to date, and intend to plant 750,000 more over the next few years. Eventually, on some parts of Ocean Beach, a continuous swathe of native vegetation will extend from the shoreline to the top of the coastal cliff faces, a sight now seldom seen in the North Island.

In 2013, the Department of Conservation recognised the Ocean Beach dune system as one of New Zealand's top 50 habitats, not only for its ecological importance but for the biological history in the sands. Tamsin Ward-Smith describes the area as being, 'like a history book of what was there once – from moa and all sorts of other species, such as

New Zealand ravens and so on, that are extinct, but also birds that are still alive but no longer there ... even Fiordland penguins. They have been gone for so long that they have become Fiordland crested, but perhaps they were once Cape penguins. You can still pick up bits of eggshell that are curved and porous, and you know they were from something big because of the shape of the piece.'

The dunes and the lands behind them are also an invaluable source for archaeologists and historians. Hundreds of midden heaps and various other archaeological sites provide information about Māori houses, diet, food preparation, storage pits, gardens, tools, rituals and burial customs. Bone and eggshell fragments also found in the dunes show clearly that Cape Kidnappers had once been home to a wide range of native species, although many are now either extinct altogether or confined to predator-free offshore islands. For McLennan, the dunes are 'full of treasures, with stories about the past and present that are worth preserving.'

REINTRODUCING NATIVE BIRDS: CONTROVERSY AND SURPRISES

Once the fence was built, a programme of reintroducing native birds immediately commenced. The first species released, North Island robins, were sourced from Maungataniwha

OPPOSITE
Overlooking the dunes, with the predator-proof fence going down to Ocean Beach.

forest, where the owner, Simon Hall, is also committed to conservation and pest eradication. Tomtits, whiteheads and then riflemen followed. By 2014, the population of 44 robins originally transferred had grown to more than 70 pairs; the tomtits had expanded to 200 pairs, and there were numerous flocks of whiteheads and more than 10 pairs of riflemen. Tamsin Ward-Smith recalls: 'The robins, tomtits and the whiteheads came from pine forest, so they had lived in pine forest before, but we thought by bringing them out to the Cape, they would love to return to the native forest there. Well, we let them go and literally within a few days a lot of them were turning up in the pine trees. They actually chose the pine trees, and flew from the native to the pine trees. So we were surprised there. It wasn't what we'd expected.'

In 2009, a more controversial translocation took place – of New Zealand's rarest duck: the pāteke or brown teal. Many conservationists believed the Cape Sanctuary to be an unsuitable environment for this species: it was too dry, too populated by predators, and lacked forest cover. The Pāteke Recovery Group, which advises on the national management of the species, remained completely divided about the proposed transfer plan. But fossil deposits in the dunes, which proved that pāteke had previously

ABOVE
Pāteke making themselves at home.
CAPE SANCTUARY COLLECTION

inhabited the Cape, finally helped to convince the initial doubters.

John McLennan remembers that the pāteke translocation was 'a very divisive issue' for a time: 'It became a whole test for New Zealand conservation. So the pāteke came in here and people watched with bated breath and we monitored them really, really closely . . . and to everyone's astonishment, they did amazingly well. We had thought they would do all right, but we just didn't believe they would take off in the way they did. We now have them turning up in ponds outside of the sanctuary . . . they've gone far and wide: it's just fantastic.'

The first introduction of 15 pairs in 2008 proved so successful that more pāteke were translocated to the sanctuary over the next two years. With an 80 per cent survival rate, and abundant chicks each year, their population has grown to about 200 ducks, with some 30–50 either straddling the sanctuary boundary or living outside of it. Pāteke have been found nesting in tussock in the golf-course turning area, seemingly oblivious to the busy comings and goings of guests and golfers. Several have also taken up permanent residence on Taurapa, the adjoining farm.

A KIWI SUCCESS STORY

Reintroducing kiwi to Cape Kidnappers is another of the sanctuary's great success stories. As with pāteke, the plan generated considerable controversy at the outset. Those arguing against it claimed that the property was too dry and that no kiwi lived on the east coast of the North Island. But, as John McLennan points out, studies of the Ocean Beach dunes proved that brown kiwi had lived there in the past and, again, that helped to sway opponents: 'The dune studies of [Trevor] Worthy helped enormously. Without the subfossil evidence, we would have been unable to convince some people that pāteke and kiwi, now largely confined to wet habitats, could actually live in places as dry and drought-prone as the Cape. There were many times in the early years of the sanctuary's development that I mentally thanked Trevor Worthy for the detective work he had done at Ocean Beach.'

The first kiwi, some 23 birds sourced from four locations in Hawke's Bay, were introduced into the sanctuary in 2008 and 2009.

More arrived over the next few years. The survival rate was very good. Tamsin Ward-Smith observes with justifiable pride that, 'there are probably up to 100 adult birds out at the Cape now.' Again, like the other birds, Ward-Smith recalls: 'Kiwi filled up the pine forest first, and only now that is reaching capacity with kiwi and other species are they moving into the native – they are going back across the road into the native side. It's not what you would expect. So we have learned a lot.'

To everyone's surprise and amusement, kiwi have even spread out to the irrigated golf course: 'You find that kiwi do absolutely fine on the golf course, for example. They are snuffling around the bunkers and causing havoc! It all shows how adaptable wildlife is. You can have wildlife and people and recreation and tourism and farming and all that together. They are doing really well despite concerns in the early days that it was too dry for them and they weren't going to cope in the droughts we have out here.'

Even John McLennan, who fought fiercely to bring kiwi to the sanctuary, has been surprised at their remarkable adaptability: 'When you look at the brown kiwi, most of them are in the remote ranges

ABOVE
Kiwi.

OPPOSITE
Tamsin Ward-Smith releasing kiwi chicks with Andy Lowe, watched by Paratene te Huia.

of New Zealand and they are always high-rainfall areas. So people begin to think of them living in those wet areas. When we took them down to the Cape I was a bit unsure about how well they would do in that dry summer landscape. I was genuinely surprised to find out that they were drought-tolerant – extraordinarily drought-tolerant. That was a lovely surprise.'

The Cape Sanctuary continues to work closely with the Kaweka Eco Ed project, the Westshore Kiwi House, Ruahine Forest Park and Maungataniwha forest owned by Simon Hall, on the kiwi restoration programme. To protect the young chicks from predators, eggs are taken from the forest after about 60–70 days of natural incubation and transferred to Kiwi Encounter in Rotorua to hatch. They then come to the Cape as chicks to be released. As Ward-Smith explains: 'They are crèched at the Cape. Maungataniwha [and the Kaweka and Ruahine Ranges] is not pest-free. There is no fence, and, although they do a lot of trapping work, there is a good chance that young chicks would get eaten by stoats and the like. We send some kiwi back at about 800–1000 grams – which is the weight at which most young birds are better able to fight off stoats, and we keep half here to seed the Cape. The whole system has worked really well for all involved: everybody and every kiwi benefit.'

In its short existence, according to McLennan, '[The] Cape Sanctuary has made a significant and valuable contribution to kiwi conservation in Hawke's Bay . . . '

OPPOSITE
John McLennan tracking kiwi with two schoolboys.

In 2009, McLennan and his wife, Sue, developed Kiwi Discovery Walks for the lodge guests. The activity is a 'win-win' for all involved. As McLennan observes: 'You have this upmarket lodge with visitors from all over the world turning up at exactly the same time the chicks are there, and the chicks have to be checked on a pretty regular basis. The guests are taken to the site, given the details of each chick and then – and this is the key to the success of it, they are not observers, they become participants; it makes a huge difference. We dial up the transmitting number on the receiver, give them the aerial and send them off to find the chick – they become wildlife managers for a couple of hours, they learn to track.'

The walks proved such a hit that John and Sue could no longer manage them on their own: 'Last summer we did 83 days in a row, and some of those days were 5am in the morning until dark. It started slowly and then became so popular, it even got to the point where other upmarket lodges were phoning us and asking us to provide them with the same service, because they would get guests from Cape

ABOVE
Young kākā.
CAPE SANCTUARY COLLECTION

OPPOSITE TOP
Kākā in aviary.

OPPOSITE BOTTOM
Kākāriki.
ENA CONWAY

Kidnappers who were saying it was the best thing they had done in New Zealand. It got to the point where we couldn't cope, so now it has been taken over by the sanctuary staff.'

In addition to kiwi, the abundant birdlife on the property delights guests at the lodge. In November and December, a time when visitors from the northern hemisphere often visit, pōhutukawa and flax flowers in the gardens attract a dazzling concentration of tūī and bellbirds. To find honeyeaters of this size in such large numbers on the Cape is a significant achievement, as normally only New Zealand's predator-free offshore islands would offer such a sight. In the evenings, the golf course comes alive with birdlife. As John McLennan's 2013 report on the Cape Sanctuary notes: 'Family groups of pāteke shower under the irrigation sprinklers, and kiwi feed on porina grubs in the rough pastures bordering the fairways.'

PARAKEETS AND PARROTS

In August 2012, Cape Sanctuary volunteers designed and constructed an aviary for kākāriki (parakeets) and kākā (parrots). Positioned in forest in the top corner of the Rough Block, this facility is an easy 10-minute walk from the lodge. Julian Robertson's Aotearoa Foundation supplied funds to Poutiri Ao ō Tāne – a collaborative ecological and social restoration project located at the Maungaharuru Tutira catchment, 60 kilometres north of Napier. Poutiri Ao ō Tāne then forwarded funds for half of the Cape Sanctuary aviary costs. Local suppliers donated materials, and volunteers gave freely of their time and labour.

In 2012, 44 red-crowned kākāriki were successfully translocated into the sanctuary from Kapiti Island. Kākāriki have also been successfully bred in captivity, both in the aviary and elsewhere, and then released into the sanctuary. These lively, vividly green-coloured birds, once abundant but now in severe decline except on predator-free offshore islands, are enormously popular inhabitants of the sanctuary. Many are tame enough to be fed by hand, and they roam as far afield as Havelock North.

ABOVE
Cook's petrel chicks
CAPE SANCTUARY COLLECTION

SEABIRD RESTORATION AND SHOREBIRD REVIVAL: MAKING 'CONSERVATION HISTORY'

In his 2013 Cape Sanctuary report, John McLennan described the almost complete annihilation of mainland colonies of burrowing seabirds as 'the most consequential effect of introduced mammals in New Zealand. Within a few decades, cats, rats and stoats destroyed entire breeding colonies of burrowing seabirds whose inhabitants numbered in the millions.'

Thanks to a grant from the Government Biodiversity Condition Fund in 2008, a predator-proof fence was built around a former seabird breeding colony within the sanctuary. The site, perched on a cliff-top, is difficult for people to reach, but the soils are burrow-friendly and the cliff offers a perfect launching-off spot for young petrels. Transfers of the first nestlings from offshore islands – grey-faced petrel, Cook's petrel and diving petrel – enjoyed a 96 per cent fledging rate. This spectacular success encouraged many more transfers. In a 2010 article for *Forest and Bird*, Christine Fallwell described the transfer of 50 'soft-grey, downy-coated' Cook's petrel nestlings to the Cape Sanctuary as having made 'conservation history'.

By the completion of the six-year transfer programme in December 2014, a total of 490 grey-faced petrel chicks had successfully translocated. Tamsin Ward-Smith explains: 'The grey-faced petrels go off to sea for seven years, and the Cook's petrel are away for about four years on the ocean or doing whatever they have been doing. Cook's petrel migrate all the way to Alaska and then come back. Adult seabirds are just beginning to come back now, and it is so exciting as you are not sure if it has worked, then all of these pairs come back . . . At the burrow entrances we put up sticks like little chopsticks, and as the birds come back they knock the sticks down – that is how we know they've returned. We also put up infrared cameras so we have got them on camera as well, coming and going.'

ABOVE
Feeding a petrel chick.
CAPE SANCTUARY COLLECTION

> At the burrow entrances we put up sticks like little chopsticks, and as the birds come back they knock the sticks down – that is how we know they've returned.

In addition to translocated seabird species, a wide range of shorebirds have reintroduced themselves to the Cape and its environs in the wake of dune protection and predator control. These include, among others, red-billed gulls, white-fronted terns, oystercatchers, pied stilts, and reef herons. The rare and endangered New Zealand dotterel increased from one breeding pair in 2006 to nine pairs in 2010, with annual chick production soaring from zero to 18 over the same period.

Little blue penguins have also been encouraged to return to the dunes by the placement of nesting boxes in areas where they are known to breed. The boxes are necessary, according to Ward-Smith, because: 'When I first started [managing the sanctuary], the only penguins I found were dead ones, chewed up by a predator or washed up on the beach. They have always been in the waters around Hawke's Bay, but were probably not doing particularly well, as there was not much habitat for them to roost in. There is not a lot of cover along that coast at the moment. But that is changing, by excluding the stock and new planting. We have placed over 300 boxes for them to come and nest in, which they are using to burrow in when they come onto land.'

The New Zealand shore plover, with only 120 remaining, is one of the world's rarest waders. Helping to restore their numbers will be a future focus at the Cape Sanctuary. 'We are going to breed them in aviaries at Ocean Beach and let them go free at other locations, and hopefully one day here at the Cape.'

TWO SPECIAL GIFTS

'Conservation Milestone': Takahē at the Cape

On 14 September 2012, representatives from four South Island runanga (councils) – Awarua, Waihopai, Hokonui and Oraka/Aparima – and the Takahē Recovery Group administered by the Department of Conservation delivered the first of four pairs of takahē to the Cape Sanctuary. According to the 2013 Cape Sanctuary report, this event was 'undoubtedly the most significant conservation milestone in the history of the sanctuary thus far', one that 'clearly signified that both iwi and the Department of Conservation were willing to entrust private individuals with some of the country's rarest species.'

Since then, there have been further translocations; there are currently eight takahē in the sanctuary, and one pair bred last summer.

Tuatara Return to the Cape

In early 2012, South Island iwi Ngāti Koata of Te Tau Ihu gifted 20 juvenile tuatara to Ngāti Mihiroa of Heretaunga. Ngāti Koata and Ngāti Mihiroa together then asked the landowners of the Cape Sanctuary if the reptiles could be released in the sanctuary. Under the terms of the proposed translocation, Ngāti Koata would retain ownership of the tuatara and their offspring in perpetuity, while the sanctuary would facilitate the safe return of tuatara to a part of the country where they had previously lived for centuries. The landowners accepted Ngāti Koata and Ngāti Mihiroa's request with delight, recognising this gift as both a special honour and a significant event in the history of the Cape Sanctuary, for, until the past 150 to 200 years, tuatara had always been there.

Placed into a special enclosure within the seabird site, the young tuatara thrived. Ngāti Koata gifted 40 more mature adult tuatara to Ngāti Mihiroa and the Cape Sanctuary in October 2012. Released into another enclosure within the seabird cell, these adults also flourished. Ward-Smith is confident that the tuatara in the sanctuary 'are growing well, they are almost to capacity and we think they bred last year. They are being kept in this area and won't be released out of there until we can get rid of mice, because mice eat their eggs and their babies, and we still have mice throughout the property. We rarely handle the tuatara, but we have some houses where people can lift up the lids and have a look.'

OPPOSITE TOP
Pōwhiri led by Dave Stone.
CAPE SANCTUARY COLLECTION

OPPOSITE BOTTOM
Opening the takahē boxes.
CAPE SANCTUARY COLLECTION

ABOVE
Julian Robertson holding a tuatara.

VOLUNTEERS AND COMMUNITY

The Cape Sanctuary is a private initiative situated on private land, largely funded by the Robertson and Lowe families, with additional bits of funding coming from government agencies, special projects, philanthropists and individuals. It has gained enthusiastic support, in the form of volunteers from a number of organisations, local iwi, Hawke's Bay Regional Council, the Department of Conservation, and the general community. School groups, individuals and groups from New Zealand and overseas visit the sanctuary, while staff frequently make presentations to local schools and to a variety of local and national groups. University students undertake field trips to the sanctuary, and several have completed research projects about aspects of its work for postgraduate degrees.

Volunteers have embraced the sanctuary with open arms, and are crucial to many of its most significant achievements. Tamsin Ward-Smith now has a database of 500 keen volunteers: 'When I send out an email asking for help I get instant replies, even at odd times of the day and night. Each day we have the equivalent of about three full-time people on duty. They are all different people – all ages and stages – all with very different skills. They are so helpful: most seem to love the opportunity to help.'

This unpaid army of workers undertake a huge range of tasks, including transporting kiwi eggs and chicks, checking predator traps and bait stations, building and installing seabird burrows and nesting boxes, planting, weeding, caring for seabird chicks, building, painting, monitoring young birds and tuatara, feeding, cutting up bait, monitoring bait stations, and much more.

A prime example of volunteers' dedication is during the seabird-chick translocation programme, when they provide the backbone support necessary to care for and raise 100–170 seabird chicks until they fledge. The work involves 6am starts to prepare 8 litres of sardine 'smoothie', and a bumpy 8-kilometre ride to the seabird site, which 'can be pretty rough if it rains'.

Volunteer John Berry describes a wet trip: 'I have had some pretty exciting trips up there, slid off the road a couple of times . . . When they had that storm about three years ago, we had one bird left to feed and I went up with a friend of mine on the quad bike and there was water up to the seat of the bike. We got there and fed the bird . . . There were slips coming down everywhere. That was after the weather bomb which was pretty devastating out there.'

Once arrived, the volunteers then have eight hours of hand-feeding. It is hard work in searing summer heat. Nonetheless, volunteers remain undeterred and return year after year. John McLennan believes the seabird restoration scheme simply could not have happened without such assistance: 'I can't tell you how much work has gone into it. The community just poured out and helped us.'

Reasons for volunteering are many and varied. According to Ward-Smith, 'When you talk to volunteers about why they do it, it is interesting. Nearly all have some association with the Cape in some way: they used to go on holiday nearby, or they grew up there. Some come from Palmerston North, from Taupo, from all over. They all have their own areas and ideas.'

'When you talk to volunteers about why they do it, it is interesting. Nearly all have some association with the Cape in some way.'

John Berry, who is a bee-keeper by profession, has volunteered on many Department of Conservation projects. He became a volunteer at the sanctuary because 'I already knew Tamsin, I loved birds and I loved the outdoors. As time went on, I was helping with this and helping with that; you get involved with everything. I probably now do a total of a month a year. I would probably be one of the keener volunteers . . . There is an amazing amount of skills between the different people, but there is something for everybody and everybody learns. There is a whole community of volunteers out there and you get to know many of them . . .'

He also believes you gain more skills and interests by volunteering: 'I have always been a bush bird person; conservation of the bush and bush birds are my passion, not so much seabirds. But because we've had seabirds, and I have helped with them, the seabirds have been a big learning curve for me: you get really involved with them.'

From the outset, local iwi have supported and worked on behalf

Paratene te Huia of Ngāti Mihiroa

Paratene, a kaumātua of Ngāti Mihiroa, lived at Ocean Beach and was involved in the sanctuary from the outset. He played a particularly vital part in facilitating the native bird transfers. Without him, it would have been almost impossible because, as John McLennan explains: 'Native birds can only be transferred with iwi support both from the iwi that are receiving the gift and the iwi that are making it. So there is a lot of iwi-to-iwi communication required and Paratene led the charge for us. He was fantastic. He really did represent the sanctuary and local people well.'

John and Paratene travelled around New Zealand together over a period of about four years, visiting local iwi, requesting, discussing and explaining

ABOVE
Memorial to Paratene overlooking Ocean Beach.
CAPE SANCTUARY COLLECTION

OPPOSITE
Paratene releasing a bird at the sanctuary.
CAPE SANCTUARY COLLECTION

the implications of translocations. Once a transfer gift was agreed, the iwi responsible for the gift would accompany it, and there would be a formal exchange welcoming them to the rohe (land) of Ngāti Mihiroa. Paratene would lead that welcome, unless the gift was of great significance, such as the tuatara or takahē, then the chief of Ngāti Kahungunu would lead the proceedings.

Follow-up transfers were less important, as the gift had already been acknowledged, but nonetheless Paratene always went to the trouble of being there to welcome each introduction. Tamsin Ward-Smith remembers calling Paratene about a rifleman to be released in the sanctuary and his immediate response: '"I am on my way." And so just the two of us met and then bumped down into the Rough Block to bless and release one rifleman. He had driven all the way from Hastings to be there to send one bird on its way. Para had a unique way of bringing us all together for the good of conservation and of people.'

Paratene died very suddenly in November 2012. In recognition of his integral role in the development of the sanctuary, Liz and Andy Lowe placed a carved pou on a ridge in the sanctuary looking out to sea in his honour.

of the sanctuary. For many years, the late Paratene te Huia of Ngāti Mihiroa together with John McLennan, negotiated with those iwi whose native species they hoped to translocate to the sanctuary.

David Stone, also of Ngāti Mihiroa, is another notable supporter of the sanctuary's programmes who actively works on its behalf. Hariata Baker and her daughter Dawn Bennett, who are descendants of Anglican Bishop Frederick Bennett, have been a huge help to the sanctuary. John McLennan describes Hariata as 'an iwi leader of national significance', who has been instrumental in getting sanctuary staff to talk to the right people: 'When you are dealing with iwi, very often you don't know if you are dealing with the person who is going to make the decision, you often end up talking to the wrong person. Hariata cut through all of that she made sure that the decision-makers were going to be in the room when we talked about things, and that saved us an immense amount of time.'

ABOVE
Hariata Baker.
CAPE SANCTUARY COLLECTION

In late 2011, Hariata organised a hui to include iwi elders from the various places around New Zealand from which the sanctuary was interested in sourcing birds. 'She has such status,' McLennan observes, 'that when she says please be there next Saturday they come from all over New Zealand. It was incredibly impressive.'

This hui, in McLennan's view, was 'a watershed moment in the development of the sanctuary, with iwi leaders agreeing to support it.'

As the Department of Conservation and iwi have a joint management responsibility for native wildlife, consultation concerning any translocation is essential. In the case of takahē, McLennan points out that it was 'a really, really big issue nationwide, where there are so few breeding pairs . . . All of the wild ones reside in Ngāi Tahu lands, and they were very, very serious about being involved in takahē conservation. In that case, negotiations with iwi have become more important than those with DOC.'

Similarly, brown kiwis came from lands owned and administered by iwi at the northern tip of the Ruahine Ranges, so those iwi were involved from the very beginning: 'When we released them at Cape Sanctuary in I think it was August 2008, it was a huge event, in terms of people, volunteers coming out, and iwi were represented there in force; it was very symbolic for them as well.'

CAPE TO CITY: SPREADING OUT

Cape to City, another 'pioneering environmental restoration project' in Hawke's Bay, launched in May 2015. It is a collaborative partnership between Hawke's Bay Regional Council, the Department of Conservation, Landcare Research, Julian Robertson's Aotearoa Foundation, the Cape Sanctuary, as well as other Crown Research Institutes and private businesses. Andy Lowe explains, 'Cape to City is a voluntary restoration project, spread across 26,000 hectares of farmland between Waimarama and Havelock North, aimed at introducing low-cost, large-scale predator control, and it's all about economic, social and environmental sustainability. It's about pulling the three together, and it's about giving the farmers, through research and technology, a low-cost option, or at least no more than what it costs now for controlling ferrets, stoats, cats, weasels and, in some places, rats. The farmers like it. We are looking at wireless technology and long-term baits so that it is no more work for farmers, so you don't have to check every trap.'

Andy explains that 'the Cape to City vision started 10 to 12 years ago when I met John Scott who had set up the Maraetotara Tree Trust, whose object is to create a "healthier river system".'

According to the trust's website, it aims to do this by 'removing willows, fencing off covenanted riverside margins and planting these with native trees . . . to establish a lush corridor the full length of the Maraetotara River . . . to improve the ecosystem and to establish permanent reserved habitats for regenerating native plants, birds and wildlife'.

During that initial stage, Andy states, 'We weren't going to have a vermin-proof fence, we were just going to have big widespread vermin control with the Maraetotara Tree Trust creating a corridor for birds

'. . . If we have to build another fence in 20 to 30 years' time, we have failed, so Cape to City is all about pushing out what we have done at the Cape and making it the start of a pest-free New Zealand.'

AN 'ASTONISHING EVOLUTION'

Robert and Charlotte Fisher have described the various transformations of Summerlee/Kidnappers over the past 22 years as 'an astonishing evolution', observing: 'Who could have foretold the destiny of not only the land but of the myriad people involved. From a sheep station in dire straits to a massive restoration programme – a beautiful homestead enjoyed by hundreds of guests and a major tourist destination to the Cape through Gannet Safaris. Then, the creation of a world-class golf course, a luxury lodge, a predator-proof fence and the introduction of special native birds, including the kiwi, and recently the tuatara. The list of bird species is exhaustive, and now the sanctuary has the greatest diversity of birds on any mainland coast in New Zealand, including Fiordland.'

What sets Cape Sanctuary apart from other conservation projects in New Zealand is not only the fact that it is a private initiative, entirely on private land, largely privately funded, but also the fact that livestock farming, forestry and tourism are also taking place on the land. As the 2013 Cape Sanctuary report noted: 'The intent of the landowners, to integrate economic and conservation objectives in a multiple use landscape, has well and truly been achieved.'

John McLennan believes that 'Cape Sanctuary has got momentum, it is unstoppable now. It had a bit of a fragile beginning because a lot of people felt that trying to take biodiversity restoration in a dry landscape like the Cape was largely a waste of conservation dollars, and now those people who were very critical can see what is possible. So it has got a lot more support than it did in those early days.' Residents as far away as the coastal townships north of Cape Kidnappers are reporting more birds in their gardens.

OPPOSITE
Travis Cullen giving a presentation on predators, watched by Andy, Liz and Hunter Lowe.

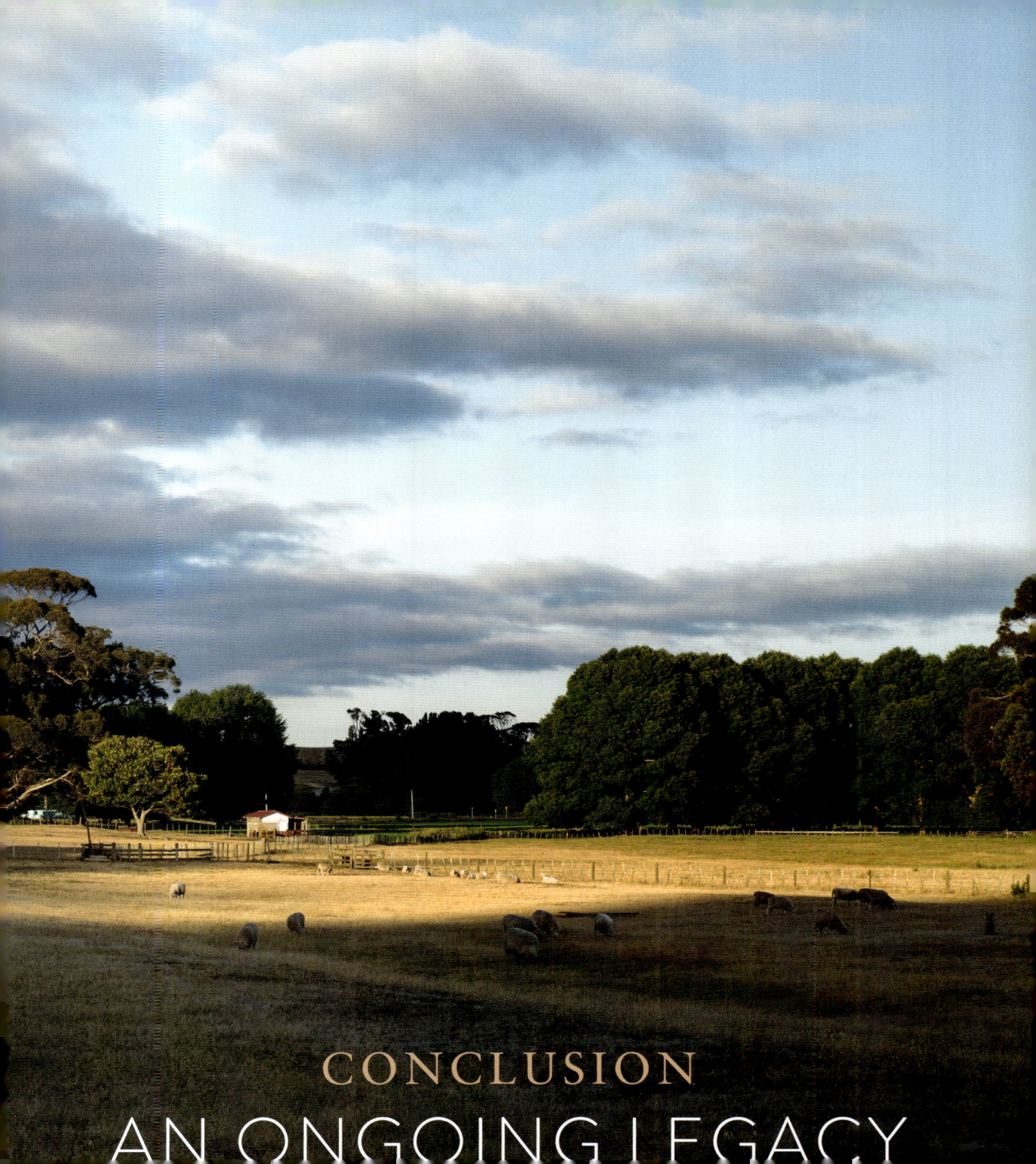

CONCLUSION
AN ONGOING LEGACY

The legacy of Clifton has changed and evolved over time, but it has endured. The original station of 5260 hectares has become 800. Two blocks have been carved off for family members, and the Cape Kidnappers block has been sold. While farming is still the core activity of these farms, Haupouri, Taurapa and Cape Kidnappers have, like Clifton, adapted and diversified in order to survive. They have all initiated adjunct activities that enable them to prosper, including tourism, forestry, horse-breeding, cropping, a café, a golf course and lodge, and a wildlife sanctuary.

At Clifton, Angus, the fifth generation of the Gordon family to farm there, has a strong sense of history, and of a commitment to the land. He sees his role on the station both as a responsibility and as part of an ongoing continuum. From the outset, he has aimed to pass Clifton on to his children in as good a condition as when he commenced farming it.

Over the years, he has had to cope with plummeting wool and sheep prices, severe droughts and floods, extensive erosion, and even the threat of the house being swept away by a massive landslide. His tenacity and ability to change course to meet the demands of a rapidly changing farming environment have enabled him to preserve this unique corner of Hawke's Bay for future generations of the family. He feels a sense of wonder towards the land, along with a sense of gratitude at being able to act as its guardian.

His wife, Dinah, shares his love of the property, and has added to and maintained the magnificent garden and, following in the footsteps of her predecessors, has kept a warm, welcoming open home for the wider family.

OPPOSITE
Four generations of Gordons at Clifton, from left: Dinah, Angus, Barbara, Tom, Lucy with Frankie, Abby.

Their son, Tom, shares the same passion for the land and for the lifestyle it provides: 'I love the historical aspect to living at Clifton, the way our family has always farmed here. I love the physical work, being out on the farm, the beauty of our environment.'

But he also realises that to be able to live there he will have to continue to diversify into other activities. 'That is why we are developing tourism, as we see it as the future of this area. One thing we are doing is setting up "glamping" on the farm so that other people can come and enjoy the environment our family has enjoyed for decades.'

> **'I love the historical aspect to living at Clifton, the way our family has always farmed here. I love the physical work, being out on the farm, the beauty of our environment.'**

While continuing to farm conventional sheep and beef, he and his wife, Lucia, are also branching into less traditional farming practices like organics, 'to cater to the demands of the growing market'.

Tom and Lucia, like the generations that have preceded them, will 'do what we have to, to continue living here – Clifton is about the joy of living here'.

OPPOSITE
Glamping overlooking the Maraetotara River.

BIBLIOGRAPHY

BOOKS

Gary Baines with Craig MacErlich, *Clive*, Clive Charitable Historic Trust Inc, 2013.

JC Beaglehole, *The Journals of Captain James Cook on His Voyages of Discovery*, vol. 1, *The Voyage of the* Endeavour *1768–1771*, Cambridge, Hakluyt Society Reprint 1988.

Mary Boyd, *City of the Plains: A History of Hastings*, Victoria University Press, Wellington, 1984.

JDH Buchanan, ed. DR Simmons, *The Māori History and Place Names of Hawke's Bay*, AW and AH Reed, Wellington, 1973.

Burden Family, *Te Awanga, our Home: Burden childhood days*, Hastings, 2009.

MDN Campbell, *Story of Napier 1874–1974: Footprints Along the Shore*, Napier City Council, Napier, 1975.

Dean Cowie, *Rangahaua Whanui District 11b, Hawke's Bay*, Waitangi Tribunal Rangahaua Whanui Series, Wellington, 1996.

Angus Gordon, *In the Shadow of the Cape: A History of the Gordon Family of Clifton*, Hawke's Bay, 2004 [self-published].

Kay Mooney, *History of the County of Hawke's Bay*, Hawke's Bay County Council, vol. 1, Hastings, 1973.

Anne Salmond, *Between Worlds: Early Exchanges between Māori and Europeans, 1773–1815*, University of Hawaii Press, 1997.

JG Wilson, *History of Hawke's Bay*, Reed, Dunedin, 1939.

Matthew Wright, *Havelock North: The History of a Village*, Hastings District Council, Hastings, 1996.

Matthew Wright, *Hawke's Bay: The History of a Province*, Dunmore Publishing Ltd, Palmerston North, 1994.

Matthew Wright, *Town and Country: The History of Hastings and District*, Hastings District Council, Hastings, 2001.

(Nicolette) Alison Wright, *William Morris, Master Whaler 1815–1882, from Blackrock, Co. Cork to Hawkes Bay New Zealand*, Hawkes Bay, 2004 [self-published].

(Nicolette) Alison Wright, *William Morris Daybook, Life in Early Port Ahuriri*, 2004 [self-published].

OTHER PRINT SOURCES

'$5.3m gift sets up Antarctic research unit', *New Zealand Herald*, 21 August 2012.
'Philanthropist's long love affair with country', *New Zealand Herald*, 12 March 2012.
Judy Lee, 'Life's a Bach at Te Awanga', *Hawke's Bay Today*, 20 March 2004.
John McLellan, Cape Sanctuary Te Matau-a-Māui Report, 2008–13, December 2013.
Calida Smylie, Spotlight on Hawke's Bay, 'Food and wine draws in the crowds', *NBR*, 2 November 2015.
Audrey Young, 'A Kiwi Knight to Remember', *New Zealand Herald*, 13 August 2011.

ONLINE SOURCES

Te Ara: the encyclopedia of New Zealand – www.teara.govt.nz
Papers Past – www.paperspast.natlib.govt.nz
New Zealand Electronic Text Collection – www.nzetc.victoria.ac.nz – online version of Turton's *Māori Deeds of Land Purchases in the North Island of New Zealand*, vol. 2.
Department of Conservation – www.doc.govt.nz
Statistics New Zealand – www.stats.govt.nz/Census.aspx

FAMILY SOURCES

Gordon Family Papers
Hill Family Diary, courtesy of Peter Hill

INTERVIEWS

Barbara Gordon, Angus Gordon, Dinah Gordon, Serena Gordon, Lionel and Pat Wilkin, Charlotte and Robert Fisher, Jo Fisher, Andy Lowe, Tamsin Ward-Smith, John McLennan, John Berry.

ACKNOWLEDGEMENTS

First and foremost the authors are indebted to Angus Gordon's *Clifton, In the Shadow of the Cape: A History of the Gordon Family of Clifton*, 2004. In writing that book, Angus unearthed documents, letters, diaries and photographs and turned them into a comprehensive, entertaining history of the family and the area. This made our task immeasurably easier and saved many hours of research. Diana is particularly grateful to Angus and Dinah Gordon for their kindness and hospitality during her visit to Clifton, and for taking the time to show her around both the homestead and the station.

The contemporary history of Clifton, which features in Chapters 6 and 7, is largely based on oral or email interviews with members of the Gordon family and with Lionel and Pat Wilkin. We would like to thank Barbara Gordon, who described life at Clifton post-WWII; Angus Gordon, who brought us up to date on life, work and changes at Clifton in the 21st century; Dinah Gordon, who told us about her life at Clifton; Serena White, who vividly described growing up and working on the farm; Tom Gordon and his wife Lucia, who spoke about their present life at Clifton and their vision for its future; Lionel Wilkin, who told us in detail about his 22 years working on the farm; and Charles, Edward and Rosie Gordon, who told us stories about growing up at Clifton. We are grateful to Juliet and Warwick Hansen for taking time from a busy farming schedule to talk to us about their life and work at Haupouri, the subject of Chapter 8.

For Chapter 9, which deals with the Cape Sanctuary, we are especially indebted to Tamsin Ward-Smith, director of the sanctuary. In addition to being a fount of knowledge about its operations, she patiently and obligingly answered endless email questions and sourced photos for us. John McLennan's fascinating, comprehensive report 'Cape Sanctuary, Te Matau a Māui 2008–2013' (prepared for the Lowe and Robertson families in December 2013), provided much of the information for this chapter. John, like Tamsin, promptly answered innumerable email and phone questions and was an unfailingly helpful mine of information. Andy Lowe filled us in on the origins of the sanctuary, and his PA Amanda Bean responded

ACKNOWLEDGEMENTS

ABOVE
The extended Gordon family at Tom and Lucia's wedding.

efficiently to all our requests for various bits of information, as well as maps. Thanks too to John Berry, who told us what it is like to work as a volunteer at the sanctuary.

We are also very grateful to Charlotte and Robert Fisher for their information about Summerlee, Jo Fisher, who described her work as a driver for the Gannet Safaris, and Julian Robertson, who explained the origins of the golf course. Sam Howard was an enthusiastic and knowledgeable source of information about the Clifton County Cricket Club.

Thanks to research librarians at MTG Napier, Alexander Turnbull Library, and Archives New Zealand, and to David Verran, Team Leader, Auckland Research Centre, Marleene Boyd, Librarian, New Zealand Maritime Museum, and Cathy Marr, Principal Research Analyst, Waitangi Tribunal, who helped answer research questions about Clifton's early years. We are grateful to Peter and Marcia Hill for kindly loaning us photographs and Elizabeth Hill's diaries, and to Michael Gordon for allowing us to use his photographs of Taurapa.

Special thanks to Richard Brimer for his amazing photographs, and to the talented project team at Penguin Random House: non-fiction publisher Alex Hedley, project editor Tessa King, editor Nicola McCloy, proof-readers Kate Stone and Andrea Coppock and designer Kate Barraclough.

Finally, we are grateful to our respective spouses, Rick Carlyon and John Morrow, for their ongoing encouragement and support.

INDEX

Page numbers in bold denote images

Abraham, Suresh 210
aerial top-dressing 170–1
Ahuriri 38, 40, 43, 57
  Lagoon 140
AL Elder and Co 82–3, 87
Allan, David 134
Aotearoa Foundation 247, 276, 287
Awarua runanga 279

Bachelors' Cottage **74**, 84
Baker, Hariata 286
Balance, John 88
Bay View *see* Petane
Begg S 58
Bennett, Dawn 286
Bennett, Frederick 286
Berry, John 282, 283
Black Bridge **77**
Black Reef 15, 28, **30–1**, 54, 74, 237, 241
Bostock, Ben 222
Bostock, John 200
Braithwaite 64
British Red Cross 124
Bull Brothers 94
Burden family camp 106
Butler, Tom 174

Campbell, Elizabeth (Bessie) 88
Campbell, Hugh 46
Cape Block *see* Summerlee
Cape Kidnappers 15, 23–6, **25**, **30–1**, **32–3**, 40–1, **61**, 210, 231, 260, 264, 266
  gannet colony 207, 233, 236–7, 260
  golf course 238–9, **240**, 241, 246
  Māori legend 24, 259
  naming of 31–2
Cape Kidnappers Station 8–9, 15, 244, 293 *see also* Summerlee Homestead 26
  map of **258**
Cape Palliser 26
Cape Sanctuary 244, 263–5, 268–70, 272, 276–9, 281–8
  fauna 265–6, 268
  volunteers 282–3
Cape Turnagain 40
Carnell, Samuel 44
cattle 16–17, 73, 81, 104, 108, 136, 155, 174, 176, 179, 186, 196, 221, 231, 234, 244, 252
Chalmers, Brian **222–3**
Cheviri, Sudheesh 210
Chicklade 187
Christmas 154, 156, 189
Church of the Sacred Heart 117
Clifton Café 17, **36**, 37, **206–7**, 207–10, **208**, **209**
Clifton County Cricket Club (CCCC) 188–90, **190**
Clifton Station 7–8, 15–18, 23–4, 41, 53, 87, **96**, 101, 104, 106–7, 111, 122, 126, 169, **178–9**, 180–1, 198–9, 211, 222, 293
  camping **142**, **145**
  diversifying 198–201
  employees 92, 97, 115–16, 118, 149, 169
  fauna 53–4
  flora 15–16, 53
  founding of 23, 37
  glamping **294–5**
  Gordon Brothers 103, 108
  homestead 55–6, **57**, **59**, 65, **93**, 94, **95**, **96**, **108–9**, **110**, 111, 117, 131, 152–4, 180, **193**, 194, **202**
  income streams 17, 185–6, 199–201, 207–10, 211–12, 218, 222
  inheritance of 179, 194, 215
  map of **148**, **258**
  sale of Cape block 131, 134, 145, 179–80, 293
  size of 7, 15, 104
  subdivision of 88, 251
  woolshed 111, **165–6**, 210, **211**
Clive 42, 53, 60, 75, 102
Clive Grange Station **41**, 77, 102
Cluden House 120
Coastal Spring Lamb 254
Colenso, William 33, 38–9, 43

conservation 259–61, 263–6, 268–70, 272, 274, 276–9, 281–8
Cook, Captain James 31–3
Cooper and Holt *see* Rhodes, Cooper and Holt
cricket *see also* Clifton County Cricket Club (CCCC)
  John Gordon Memorial Cup 189
  Legends of Cricket Art Deco Match 190
Cullen, Travis 263, **289**
Cyclone Pam 204–5

Deep Creek 16
Department of Conservation 237, 263, 265, 279, 282–3, 286–7
Devon 75, 84, 92, 102, 104, 108, 120
Doak, Tom 239
dogs 15–16, 172–3
Don family 23
Donnelly, Pat 189
Drew, Lance 263
droughts 8, 17–18, 23, 58, 60, 83, 118, 174, 177, 185, 194, 196, 198, 221, 238, 254–5, 270, 293

earthquake *see* Napier earthquake
East Clive 42, 62
Ebbett 84, 97, 123–4
Edenham Station 115
Elders *see* AL Elder and Co
Eleanor 40
Endeavour 31

Farndon 119, 125, 128
  House 131
Fernhill 67, 72, 75–6
  cattle farming 73
  House 76
Finch, WP 94
Fiordland 92, 288
First World War 119–20, 122, 125, 142
  ambulance **120**
Fisher, Charlotte 9, 162, 231, 288
Fisher, Jo 233–234
Fisher, Robert 9, 231–2, 259, 288

INDEX 301

Flat Rock 26, 28
flooding 174, 176–7, 202
Forbes and Coates government 140
Fraser town 174

Gannet Beach Adventures 210, 237, 241
Gannet Safaris Overland 210, 233, **235**, **237**, 288
gannets *see* Cape Kidnappers gannet colony
Gap, The 26, 31
Gillies, Charlie 169
Glenny, Sarah 161
golf 100, 108 *see also* Cape Kidnappers golf course
Gordon Brothers 103–5, 108, 111
Gordon Family 7, 9, **154**, **155**, **156**
   Abby **14**, 161, 181, 192, **194**, 215, **216**, 292
   Angus 7–9, 13, **14**, 15–18, 37, 151, 153, **154**, **155**, **156**, 158, **159**, 161, 163, 164, 169, 171, 173, 179–81, 185–7, 188, **192**, **194**, **195**, **196**, 198–**201**, 203–5, 207, 209–10, 211–212, 212–**213**, 215–216, 218, 221–2, 292, 293
   Barbara 9, **14**, 150, **152**, **153**, **158**, 159–61, 163–4, 166, 169, 173–4, 179, 187, 215, 241, **292**
   Captain Thomas Edward 51, 63–8, 70–6, 82–4, 87, **88**, 97, 100, 102–4, 120, 124–6, 251
   Charles 153, **155**, **156**, 158, 164, 192, 241
   Charlie 15, 28, 75, 81, 87, **88**, 91–2, 94, 102, 122, 124, 131, 134, 136
   Dinah 8–9, **14**, 18, 161, **162**, 181, 189, **192**, **194**, 207, **209**, 210, 215–16, **292**, 293
   Dorothy 129, 131–2, 136, 138, 149, **150**, 159, 180, 187
   Edward 153, 164, 188–9, **192**
   Edward Robertson 15, 28, 65, **103**, 104–5, 106, 108, 111
   Eileen 86, **88**, 94, 99–100, 115, **116**, 120, 122–5, 131, **151**, 160, 179–80
   Elizabeth 23

   Elizabeth (Bessie) **88**, 91
   Ellen (Nelly) 77, **88**, 94, 96–8, 100, 102, 104–5, 108, 115–17, **116**, **117**, 145, **160**
   Evelyn (Ev) 128–9, 131
   Francesca (Frankie) **14**, 16, **222–3**, **227**, **292**
   Frank 15, 16, 65, **75**, 76, 81–8, **83**, **88**, 92, 94, 96–8, **99**, 100–105, 108, 111, 115–20, **116**, 117, 120, 122–6, **125**, 128, **129**, 131–2, 134, **135**, 136–8, **140**, 142, 145, 149–50, 160, **161**, 180, 199, 236
   Helen 65
   Ian 91, 111, 251
   Isabel Carlyon 216
   James Gillespie **22**, 23–4, 37, 40, 46, 51–4, 57–8, 62–3, 65, 67–8, 71, 73–4, 97
   Janet 63–6, 68, 71
   Jenny 153, 158, **159**, **163**, 164, 181
   John 9, 16, 131, 135–8, 145, 149–50, **150**, **151**, **152**, **153**, **156**, 159, 161, 164, 170, 172, 174, 177, 179, 185–7, 189, 194, 198–9, 215, 241
   Lily Carlyon 181, 216
   Lindsay (Thomas Lindsay) 86, **88**, 94, 99–102, 111, 115, **116**, 118–20, 122–5, 128–9, 131–132, **151**, 179–80, 251
   Lucia 9, **14**, 17–18, **222–3**, 226, **292**, 294
   Michael 58, 91, 92
   Mick 91, 111, 132, 251
   Patrick 91, 111
   Rosie 153, **154**, **163**, 164
   Rupert Carlyon 181, 216
   Serena 153, 156, **158**, **163**, 164, 169
   Tom 7, 9, **14**, 15, 16–18, 173, 181, **184**, 188, 192, **194**, **195**, 204–5, 211, 215–16, **217**, 218, **219**, 221–2, **222–3**, 226, **227**, **292**, 294
   William Cracroft 51–54, 57–8, 63, 65, 68
Gordon Farming Limited 17, 218
Government Biodiversity Condition Fund 265, 277
Grange Bridge *see* Black Bridge
Great Depression 137
Grey, Governor George 65
Guardian Trust 149

Hall, Simon 268, 272
Halliday, John 129
Halliday, Margaret 129
Hansen family 9, 260
   Bridget 252
   Hillary 252, 254
   Juliet 251–2, **253**, 255
   Warwick 251–2, **253**, 254–5
Harrow 145
Hastings 97, 107, 116–17, 119, 123, 137, 140, 142, 155, 170, 285
   Carnival Week 140
   District Council 241, 262
   Steeplechase Ball 98
   Trade Hall 140
   Women's League 140
Hauhau 68–70
Haumene, Te Ua 68
Haumoana 161, 174, 196
Haupouri 8–9, 15, **27**, 28, 29, 104, 108, 111, 123, 125, 132, 159, 251–2, 254–5, 293
   beef and sheep operation 252, 254
   homestead 255
   horse-breeding *see* New Zealand Performance Horses (NZPH)
   map of **258**
   size of 104
   stables **254–5**
   subdivision of 255, 259–60
Havelock North 62–3, 85, 102, 107, 226, 252, 276, 287
   Cemetery 145
Hawea 26
Hawke's Bay 15, 18, 23, 25, 34, 35, 40–1, 96, 128, 287
   A and P Show 97, 100
   Agricultural Society 63, 142
   Best Café award 207
   Christian missionaries 38
   Club 61–2, 67–8
   County Council 96, 115, 145
   Native Lands Alienation Commission 67

Open Golf Championship 100
Provincial Council 60
Regional Council 263, 282, 287
Repudiation Movement 67
Steam Navigation Company 58
tourism 210, 233, 237
transport and roads 58, 60–3
hay-making 164, **182–3**, 218
Heaps, Rod 241
Hemmings, Fanny 108
Heretaunga 25–6, 37, 43–4, 66–8, 281
   Plains 29, 66
Herrick family 150
   Eddie 92, 180
Hill Country Corporation 261–2
Hill family **73**, 101
   Captain Kenrick 64, 66, 71–2, 74–6
   Dudley 71, 108, 116
   Elizabeth 64, 71–2, 74
   Kathleen 71
   Nina 26
Hinerakau 29
HMS *Herald* 42
Hokonui runanga 279
Hood, Sir John 247
horses 57, 68, 73, 99–100, 104, 116, 136, 152, 156, 158, 160, 164
   see also New Zealand Performance Horses (NZPH); pony club
Howard, Sam 189–90
Howard, Van 189
hunting 66, 72, 74, 97, 100, 111, 158, 162, 192, 260

Ihungia Station 192
In the Shadow of the Cape 18, 212
Indian Mutiny 23
influenza epidemic 84, 126

Jacky Tie *see* Tiakitai

Kahungunu 26, 29
kākā **274**, **275**, 276
kākāriki **275**, 276
Kapiti Island 276
Karachi 53
Karaka Hill 26, 132, 232
Karamu 126
Kaukapakapa 116

Kauri Cliffs 238
Kauri Cliffs Golf Course 234
Kaweka Eco Ed project 272
Kaweka Range 272
Kidnapper Estate **52**
Kidnappers Run 41, 52
King Tāwhiao 44
Kinloch house 180
Kinross, JG 46, 58
Kirk, David 251, 255
kiwi 269–**70**, **271**, 276
Kiwi Discovery Walks 244, 274
Kiwi Encounter 272
Korean War 170
Kurahaupō waka 25
Kurupo Te Moananui 35

Law, Alec 149
Lindisfarne 150, 152, 159, 161
Logan, Jo 207
London 120, 124, 128
   Hospital 122
Lord Knutsford 122
Lowe family 260, 265, 282
   Lowe, Andy 9, 255, 259–64, **271**, 285, 287, **289**
   Lowe, Graham 212
   Lowe, Hunter **289**
   Lowe, Liz 285, **289**

MacFarlane 102
Mahia 15, 26, 35, 40
Major Hopkins 23
Makere 42
Maney, RD 67
Mangaterere 174, 196, 199
Māori King movement 43–4, 63, 65
Maraetotara Falls 16
Maraetotara River 23, 53, 88, 98, 102, 104, **150**, 157, 287
Maraetotara Tree Trust 287
Maraetotara valley 164, 186
Massey, WJ 237
Mataoka 51
Matarau (Mataurau) **27**, 28, 74
Mataraua *see* Matarau
Mataurau **27**, 74
Māui 24–5, 259
Maungataniwha forest 266, 268, 272
McCord, Jonathan 241

McHardy, Alexander 46
McLean, Donald 42–4, 46, 58, 70
McLean, Margaret 162
McLennan, John 263, 266, 269–70, 272, **273**, 274, 276–7, 283–4, 286, 288
McLennan, Sue 274
Meeanee 53, 60
Mohaka 43
Mortgagors and Leasees Rehabilitation Act 137
Morris Jr, William 35
Morris Sr, William 34–5, 38

Napier 15, 35, 44, 53, 58, 60, **61**, 62–4, 68, 97, 107, 132, 142
   earthquake 138–40, 210
   hospital 215
   Masonic Hotel 63
   Presbyterian Church School 62
   Race Days 62, 66
   Savings Bank 62
Napier, Jenny 194
Nee Harland, Peter 241
Neilson family 15, 231
   Neilson, Andrew 231
   Neilson, Colonel William 132, 134, 137
   Neilson, Maude 132
   Neilson, Michael 37, 231
Nelson 51–2
Nelson Brothers 81, 83
Nelson, William 81
New Zealand Performance Horses (NZPH) 251–2
New Zealand Steam Navigation Company 60
Ngāi Tahu 286
Ngaruroro River 29, 62
Ngāti Hawea 26
Ngāti Hineuru 69
Ngāti Kahungunu 26, 285
Ngāti Koata 281
Ngāti Kurukuru 26
Ngāti Mihiroa 281, 284–6
Nicol, Lewis 176
Nilsson, Matt 189
Northwood, James 42

Oamanui **69** *see also* Ōmarunui
Ocean Beach 28, 74, 92, **250**, 260,

261–2, 264–5, **267**, 269, 279, 284
Okawa 158
Olsen, Garry 149, 164
Omāhu 26
Ōmarunui 70–1 *see also* Oamanui
Oneporo Gully 64
Opōtoki 69
Oraka/Aparima runanga 279
Oreka 258
Ormond, John Davies 46, 67, 126
Orsborn, John **151**, 164, 212
Otanui 164, 180, 186–7

Pai Marire movement *see* Hauhau movement
Pakiaka 44
Panapa 59
Pari Kārangaranga 31
pāteke 268–9
Pāteke Recovery Group 268
pest control 260, 263–4
Petane 69
petrels 278
Pigeon Gully 16, 53
Pinckney, Reginald 119–20, 122, 124
pony club 161–3
Poraiti 20
Porpoise Gully 54, 66
Port Ahuriri 57
Poukawa 43
Poulton, Budge 164
Poulton, Nec 99
Pourere 42
Pouriri a o Tāne 276
Puapua *see* Flat Rock
Pulford, Frank 149, **165**, 169–70

Rabbit Gully 83, 107
race relations 44, 63, 65, 68–9
Ranga Ika 23, 43, 68, 104, **132**
  whaling 34–7, 39
recession 126, 128 *see also* Great Depression
Red Bridge 102
Renata Kawepo 69–70
Rhodes, Captain WB (William Barnard) 40–1, 42
Rhodes, Cooper and Holt 40–1
Rhodes, Joseph 34, 41, 46, 52–3
Richardson, Ian 211

Riverslea 85–6
Rissington 40
  Bridge 135
Robertson Foundation 247
Robertson, Josie 234, 247
Robertson, Julian 9, 210, 234, 238–9, **246**–7, 255–60, 276, 281, 287
Robertson, Pat 75, 99, 124
Robinson, Paul 251
Robinson, Sue 210
Rongokako 29–31
Rotorua 272
Rough Block 104, 135, 231, 259–60, 276, 285
Round Hill 16, 187
Ruahine Forest Park 272
Ruahine Range 43, 272, 287
Ruddick farm 118
Russell, Henry 46, 67
Russell, T Purvis 46, 67

Savage, Michael Joseph 140
Scinde Hill 61, 64
Scinde Island 53
Scott, John 287
Second World War 149
Shallow Creek 16
Shaw, Bill 37, 161, 189, 196, 198
sheep 8, 23, 35, 41, 46, 57, 60, 68, 72–3, 81, 84–5, 87, **89**, **91**, 96–7, 100–1, 104, 111, 115, 118, 123, 134–5, 150–**1**, 159, 164, 166, 169, **184**, 186, **214**, **218**, **219**
  shearing 87, 97, 101–2, 105, 108, 122, 164, **165**, 166, **168**, 169
  wool 8, 17, 46, 57–8, 60–1, 66, 81, 85–6, 92, 104, 124, 170, 186
Smith, Harry 101
Sommerville, Chum 105
Sommerville, John 97, **104**, 105, 118–20, 122–4, 131–2
St Hill, Dick 115, 120, 123
Stevens, George 71
Stone, Dave **280**, 286
Sturm, Frederick 100
Sturm, Rudolph 100
Success 58
Summerlee 132, **133**, 134, 156, 174, 231–4, 238, 255, 259, 288 *see also* Cape Kidnappers Station

House 132, **232**–3
  sale of 231, 234
supplementary minimum prices (SMPs) 171, 185, 195
Sutton, Frederick 67
Symonds, Bernie 171

takahē 279, **278**, 281, 286
Takahē Recovery Group 279
Takamoana, Karaitiana 44, 67, 69
Tangaroa 25
Tanner family 74
  Charlie 99, 123–4
  Ellen (Nelly) 77
  Errington 85
  Julia 66, 85–6
  Rose 101
  Thomas 64–7, 85–6
Taraia 26
Taranaki 63
Tarawera 69, 99
Tareha 69
Tareha's Bridge 60
Taurapa 15, 16, 28, **59**, 88, 91, **92**, 102, 123, 212, 251, 255, 269, 293
  Homestead 91, **92**
  map of **258**
Tayeto *see* Tiata
Te Awanga 18, 26, 73, 106–7, 161, 187, 196
Te Hapuku 43–4, **45**, 68
Te Haroto 69
Te Hauke 44
Te Hoe Station 137
te Huia, Paratene 271, 284–5, 286
Te Ika a Māui 25
Te Mata Peak **28**, 29–31
Te Matau-a-Māui 24–6, 31, 37, 41, 68 *see also* Cape Kidnappers
  sale of 43–4
Te Moananui 41, 43–4, 70
Te Rangihiroa 69
Te Reo Areare 33
Te Tau Ihu 281
Te Whatuiapiti 26
Te Wheturariki 26
The Farm at Cape Kidnappers 241, **244**, **245**
Tiakitai 35
Tiata 32–3
Tiffen, Henry 42, 58

Tokitahi, Nepia 35
Tokitia 35
Tomoana freezing works 81, **82**
Tonganui 25
Trentham Training Camp 123
Tuanui, Alex 244
tuatara **261**, **281**, 285
Tuki Tuki pony club 161
Tuki Tuki Station 64, 77
Tukituki River 29, 38, 41–2, 58, 62, 71–2, 77, 91, 102
Tupaia 32
Tupia 32–3
Tūranga *see* Gisborne
Twelve Apostles 66–7

Vanuatu property 201, 215
Völkner, Reverend Carl 69

W. Morris Wholesale and Retail Store 38
Waihopai runanga 279
Waimarama 28, 33, **34**, 35, 92, 287
Waiōhiki 26
Waipawa River 29
Waipukurau 43, 60
Waipureku 29, 40–2, 58, 62
Wairoa 35, 40, 128
Waitangi 38
Ward-Smith, Tamsin 263, 265, 268, 270, **271**, 272, 278–9, 281–3, 285
Wattie's 199
Wellington 63, 118–19
Wellwood Terrace 106
West Clive 62
Westshore Kiwi House 272
Whakapau **27**, 28
Whakapau Bluff 104, 111
Whalebone Reef 237
Whangaehu 115, 120, 174
Whanganui 254
Whataku 44
Whatonga 25
White, Serena *see* Gordon family, Serena
Whitmore, Colonel Sir George 70
Wilder, Perry 111
Wilkin, Lionel 149, 160, 164, **165**, 166, 169, 172, 174, 176–7, 186, 198
Williams and Kettle 155

wool *see* sheep wool
Worthy, Trevor 269
Wylam, Sue 207, **209**